THOSE WERE the DAYS

Praise for the book

'Edited by Ashok K. Lahiri, this book demonstrates that he is a gifted writer who can weave anecdotes into a captivating narrative. Read and enjoy.'

—**Jagdish N. Bhagwati**
University Professor (Economics, Law and International Affairs), Columbia University

'An illuminating account of our cultural and economic diversity.'

—**Shaktikanta Das**
Governor, Reserve Bank of India (RBI)

'The Finance Commission, tasked under the Constitution to administer the federal fisc, has been one of the success stories of the Indian Constitution. One of the reasons is that it has benefitted from the experience and stewardship of stalwarts right from K.C. Neogy and K. Santhanam to A.M. Khusro, Vijay Kelkar and N.K. Singh, to name just a few.

Having had a ringside view to the working of the Commission in the 1990s, the sense of camaraderie and the dedication to a cause, left an indelible impression on me. Members of the Commission—from different disciplines, varied political persuasions and economic beliefs—rose to the occasion to create a new paradigm to nudge the states away from the comfort of political compulsions. They were ultimately driven by one objective: to do the best for their nation. The after-hour conversations and events, to relieve the tedium of a long day of dry deliberations, were priceless. Dinners at which the members would indulge in enjoyable conversations, at times inoffensive near ribaldry, demonstrated the deep connection that most of them had developed working as a team as the years rolled by.

This book does a great service by showing the human side of these stalwarts whose contribution to India's continued march is hardly known to and scarcely understood by those who are not familiar with its work. I wish the book great success.'

—**Harish Salve**
Former Solicitor General of India

THOSE WERE the DAYS

Tales from the
15th Finance Commission

Edited by Ashok K. Lahiri

RUPA

Published by
Rupa Publications India Pvt. Ltd 2022
7/16, Ansari Road, Daryaganj
New Delhi 110002

Sales Centres:
Allahabad Bengaluru Chennai
Hyderabad Jaipur Kathmandu
Kolkata Mumbai

Anthology and Preface Copyright © Ashok K. Lahiri 2022

Copyright for individual pieces vests with the respective authors

Images copyright: The 15th Finance Commission

All rights reserved.
No part of this publication may be reproduced, transmitted,
or stored in a retrieval system, in any form or by any means,
electronic, mechanical, photocopying, recording or otherwise,
without the prior permission of the publisher.

The views and opinions expressed in this book are the author's own and the
facts are as reported by him which have been verified to the extent possible,
and the publishers are not in any way liable for the same.

ISBN: 978-93-5520-133-1

First impression 2022

10 9 8 7 6 5 4 3 2 1

The moral right of the author has been asserted.

Printed at Sanat Printers

This book is sold subject to the condition that it shall not,
by way of trade or otherwise, be lent, resold, hired out, or otherwise
circulated, without the publisher's prior consent, in any form of binding or
cover other than that in which it is published.

CONTENTS

Preface	*vii*
Celebrating an Experience N.K. Singh	1
Fulfilling Cherished Dreams Prem Kumari	45
Some Incredible Journeys Anoop Singh	50
Joy, Hope and Nostalgia Ajay Narayan Jha	56
Better Late Than Never Ranjana Jha	64
A Country Like No Other Ashok K. Lahiri	68
An Opportunity of a Lifetime Rita Lahiri	81
Understanding Centre-State Ties Ramesh Chand	87

A Bouquet of Sweet Thoughts ANITA BAJAR	91
An Institution That Breathes ARVIND MEHTA	94
Falling in Love with an Idea GITA MEHTA	101
Walking Down Memory Lane CHETNA BHATIA AND MUKHMEET SINGH BHATIA	109
A Stage, Unparalleled RAVI KOTA	112
A Fulfilling Agenda ANTONY CYRIAC	121
Communicating the Essence MAUSHUMI CHAKRAVARTY	126
People and Economy Power BHARAT BHUSHAN GARG	129
An Intellectual Ride KANDARP V. PATEL	133
Learning and Unlearning ADITI PATHAK	137
A Larger Sense of Purpose SHIKHA DAHIYA	143
Both Professional and Personal NITISH SAINI	153
A Memorable Tenure ANSHUMAN MISHRA	156
Unforgettable Three Years SALAM SHYAMSUNDER SINGH	160

PREFACE

Every five years, the president of India appoints a Finance Commission (FC) with a chairman and four members, who have been or are qualified to be appointed as judges of a high court; or have special knowledge of the finances and accounts of a government; or have had wide experience in financial matters and in administration; or have special knowledge of economics. After about two years of deliberations and discussions, the FC, assisted by a secretariat of some 85 technical experts and support staff, brings out a report recommending what share of the Union Government's tax revenues should be devolved to the states in the aggregate and how this aggregate should be distributed among the different states.

Beyond these specified shares, the FC also recommends grants to individual states—which are called revenue deficit grants—to bridge the normatively assessed shortfall of their revenue receipts (including the share of the Union's tax revenues) from their normatively assessed revenue expenditure. Furthermore, the FC can recommend state- and sector-specific grants, considering the needs of the states, and give other recommendations in the interest of sound finance. The FC transfers aim at equalizing the availability of public services across the country and, hence, to offset related inequities across the states.

Excitement about the FCs in the media, and among the public, leaders and bureaucrats in states, is periodic in nature. At the time of the panel's appointment, there is some buzz around the selection of the chairman and members. After its constitution, the Commission also gets some publicity during its consultative visits to the various states. Apart from this and consultations with Union Ministries and domain experts, until it generates its report and submits it to the president of India, the FC tends to spend the intervening periods in the relative secrecy of internal discussions.

Post submission, there is, once again, excitement when its report is placed in Parliament and made public. The recommendations of the FC—regarding the share of the Centre's tax revenues it has devolved to the states, the distribution of the sharable tax revenue among the states, the revenue deficit and other grants to individual states as well as the sector-specific grants—generate considerable publicity in the media and the public for a few days. After that, a FC becomes a part of history and is judged by the merits of its report and recommendations. Add the sense that it is a critical part of the success of federalism, and the imperative of ensuring equality of treatment of both the Union Government and all the states and being perceived as an independent and impartial body is key to its legacy.

Like all FCs, the 15th FC too will be judged by the report

Preface

that we have produced and the recommendations that we have given. Furthermore, like those who were part of the preceding 14 Commissions, we too are on our way to fading out. Before we do so, our chairman, Nand Kishore (N.K.) Singh, encouraged us to look beyond the numbers and write down our tales from the 15th FC. Some of us wondered at the prospect of writing down our anecdotal tales. A sombre and serious technical body like the FC writing anecdotes was an audacious idea. Would we be misconstrued? Shall we be taken as light-hearted people who did things other than just thinking about fiscal devolution and India's federal architecture?

On second thoughts, we realized that our report will be judged independently, on its merits or the lack thereof. Our tales should neither add nor detract from that evaluation. So, we embarked upon compiling stories, which this book contains.

If you simply want to know about what we recommended and why, you should focus on our four-volume report and leave these tales aside. These narratives contain vignettes of our experiences of travelling to the 28 states of our large and diverse country, and interpersonal interactions. This is not a book on history or economics or even secret deliberations within the 15th FC. It is simply one of the tales from the FC that captures the joys of working as a team, a sense of discovery of our unity in diversity and the great camaraderie that we enjoyed with leaders and civil servants in the different states.

The prospect of crunching numbers and debating fiscal balances, the effectiveness of public expenditure and the revenue effort at various levels of the government for two years may not be sources of passion and excitement. But they become just that when the numbers are finalized and publicized. The work of the FC may even appear a bit tedious to many, but in reality, is not. Federalism is still part of a history in the making. Adding to our conclusions, we hope these tales will reveal a fascinating world in the India we all live in, and make the readers look forward to what the 16th FC will do.

I hope you will enjoy our stories.

Ashok K. Lahiri
10 October 2021

CELEBRATING AN EXPERIENCE

My Tour Diary

N.K. Singh

Could there be a benediction that 'Blessed be thee, for thou shall join the Finance Commission? And if you do, I promise to show you India as you would have never seen before!'

This is what the Finance Commission (FC) experience has meant to me—a unique opportunity that allowed me to see large parts of India which, even in my many years of engagement in public policy, I was never able to do. Amidst its sheer diversity and complexity, the unity comes through so poignantly and vividly. This is not the occasion for any serious analysis of the FC, but to be more anecdotal and, perhaps, recall the pleasant aspects of visiting the states.

And, of course, engagements with the chief ministers, each one coming from a background and legacy of their own. It would not be an exaggeration to say that the chief ministers are perhaps at their 'very best' when they engage with the FC. Many of them told me that for them, the FC was a sort of lifeline which comes every five years. Each one has their own grievances, hopes and, undoubtedly, high expectations from the outcome of the Commission's recommendations.

EAST TO WEST, NORTH TO SOUTH

I could not go with the rest of the FC to Arunachal Pradesh, given some personal problems, and so my visit to the states commenced on 25 April 2018, with Assam as my first port of call. I was visiting the state after a lapse of several years, and noticed that a few things hadn't changed. Air connectivity to Guwahati was still poor and the roads to the city from the airport remained congested; I suffered despite being pampered by escort cars.

Nevertheless, there was a quantum change from what I had experienced during my last trip, in terms of road quality and, undoubtedly, in the arrangements that had been made for my visit. The cultural programme in the evening, with the mother–daughter duo of Marami Medhi and Meghranjani Medhi rendering a classical Kathak performance together, was a rare delight. Their elegance, beauty and sophistication left a lasting impression on us. To see the mother having imparted her skills to her daughter in a manner that the duo performed with such iconic precision left us in awe.

The following day, we visited the Kamakhya Temple.

Celebrating an Experience

It was a memorable and nostalgic experience from several points of view. I had promised to the presiding goddess that I would begin my engagement with the states from Assam, and that is what happened, because I had to skip Arunachal Pradesh, which was first on the list, and where the rest of the FC went. I fulfilled my commitment and paid obeisance to the deity, who blessed us in ensuring an effortless onward visit to all the states. The temple was built around the eighth century—and underwent renovations right through the fourteenth century—and is the quintessential power of the mythical Shakti, of which this represents one of the most important seats of power. It is one of the oldest among the 51 Shakti Pithas. The deity, Ma Kamakhya, is revered as the 'Bleeding Goddess', as legends abound that in June, the area around the Brahmaputra River near the temple turns red, signifying that the Goddess 'menstruates' during this period. The temple of Ma Kamakhya is seen as a celebration of the Shakti embedded within every woman. The mythical powers of the deity are truly astounding, having experienced them myself.

The then state finance minister Himanta Biswa Sarma demonstrated his experience and domain understanding of the subject we had come to discuss, having dealt with earlier FCs and being an important Bharatiya Janata Party (BJP) leader of the entire region. To me, the then chief minister Sarbananda Sonowal came across as a man in no hurry, displaying quiet dignity and efficiency. He will go a long way. His personal charms and amiability of manners enable him to win many friends. He seemed to have no rough edges or personality kinks. Overall, he enjoys a good reputation in Assam, although only time will tell us more about his administrative skills.

We then arrived in Kerala on 28 May. It was quite a coincidence that it happened to be the very day when the monsoons were about to break in Thiruvananthapuram. From the aircraft, one could see the low, hanging clouds moving towards the Indian subcontinent. The top-floor view from the Leela Hotel, where we were staying, was breathtaking. It was my first experience of witnessing a monsoon breaking over the Indian subcontinent. I had read meteorological accounts of how the monsoon begins from the southern tip of India, so to say, and thereafter makes its way northward. To any Indian, monsoon implies a new life for the agricultural cycle and other patterns of economic activity. Many Hindi films are intertwined with the rains. I remembered that the film *Lagaan* was based on the expectations and uncertainties of the monsoons. Our civilization, as we know it, centred much on the monsoons—from cropping patterns and rejuvenation of river systems, to the availability of drinking water and the recharging of groundwater aquifers. These were the very monsoon clouds which I was now seeing.

My interaction with Thomas Isaac, the knowledgeable finance minister, whom I had only known briefly, was interesting. Like all finance ministers, he pointed out the infirmities in the devolution formula. Of course, never failing to add that if more resources were to be given to the poorer states, he could hardly object as, being a good Left leader, questioning principles of equity would be ideologically imprudent! I hoped, at that time, that he meant what he said.

Celebrating an Experience

Thereafter we proceeded to Kochi, an extraordinary city for multiple reasons. After a long, congested drive, we arrived at an important religious seat—the Guruvayur Temple, about which legends abound. Believed to be around 5,000 years old, the temple is dedicated to the four-armed avatar of Lord Vishnu, also known as Guruvayurappan. The darshan was exalting.

The next day, after taking a ride in the Metro, a project we were told was financially viable, we also visited the oldest Jewish synagogue not only in India but in the entire Commonwealth of Nations. Constructed in 1567-68 by Spanish Jews, the synagogue is also known as Paradesi, meaning 'foreigners'. The four buildings comprising the synagogue are furnished with chandeliers, clock towers and Chinese hand-painted tiles. According to history books, Samuel Castiel, David Belila and Joseph Levi built the Paradesi synagogue for the flourishing Jewish community in Kochi, consisting mainly of Malabar Jews and refugees from the religious persecution of Jews in the territories controlled by the Portuguese.

I wondered as to how and why the Jewish settlements came up in India—and that too first and foremost in Kochi. Obviously, they would have taken the sea route, although there is some controversy around the path they had chosen. It is interesting to note that, it being the oldest synagogue in India, traditional rituals are still meticulously followed there. It was a great learning experience for us.

Before winding up our Kerala visit, we went to a few Panchayati Raj institutions. We realized that in the delegation of powers and functions to these institutions, Kerala was perhaps, in many ways, a model for other states to emulate. I was particularly impressed with the scientific precision with which sanitation drainage and open defecation—which were not only conquered but recycled to better economic use—had been pursued.

Then there was our visit to West Bengal, which was unique in more ways than one. First, before the trip, I had challenged Finance Minister Amit Mitra to organize a classical evening programme which could match the one we had seen in Assam. He mentioned this to Chief Minister Mamata Banerjee, who took the matter rather seriously. When Mamata gets down to something, she can be a perfectionist and a hard taskmaster. She achieved the impossible and told me that three artists, who were not even on reasonable talking terms, would jointly perform for us. This was indeed a coup! The artists included well-known classical vocalist Rashid Khan, sarod player Tejendra Narayan Majumdar, Bickram Ghosh on the tabla and playback singer Iman Chakraborty, who was the winner of the National Film Award for Best Female Playback Singer in 2017. It was quite an amazing evening with so many impresarios. The evening programme left us spellbound—not just the ensemble who had performed together, but Mamata's amazing organizational skills as well.

I also remember that for a private condolence meeting, Mamata agreed that we could travel together. Promptly thereafter, Mitra rang up to say that Mamata usually drives a small car, with no security configurations. With affection, she enquired if I would be comfortable with this. Believe me, I eagerly looked forward to this experience. She sat next to the driver and I settled down in the rear seat. As our conversation

Celebrating an Experience

became informal, I soon noticed that we encountered no traffic signals since the roads had been cleared for her, and at every traffic signal, policemen saluted her. In some ways, it was an important symbolic gesture that the chief minister travelled in a small car with next to no security paraphernalia. The point registered on me as, indeed, also her overpowering affection.

When we reached the venue for the condolence, she insisted that I walk ahead of her. We had reached towards the end of the condolence meeting. At some critical point in time, when it came to garlanding the portrait of the deceased, I was somewhat at a loss because I had carried no flowers or garland. She turned to her security and signalled, and within seconds, a wreath arrived for me to place on the portrait. She had arranged all this in advance, realizing that I would not have the time to carry a garland or acquire a wreath. I was touched that she had anticipated and planned all this in advance. Her overpowering affection and ability floored me.

I also remember that, at some point in time during the break for our meeting, she volunteered to make tea for all members of the Commission. She reminded us that if she made tea at home for herself, she could do so for her guests too! During the discussions, she zealously defended her policy of providing free water since it was a welfare state—the persistence of some of our members for a user charge had no traction with her.

The visit to West Bengal left one important impression on my mind. Mamata was quintessentially a political entity who knew what was best designed to suit her political ends. Notwithstanding her firmness on issues which were dear to her, there was a humane dimension which not many know of. The private Mamata is vastly different from her public profile of a mercurial leader.

Now from east to the west. The first impact I felt on reaching Ahmedabad, Gujarat, was that the years of Narendra Modi's governance in the state had left an indelible imprint. Everything was well planned and precise. The visit to the Secretariat itself was interesting; the building was composed of flexible compartments and had been built in record time to host the Vibrant Gujarat Global Summit 2019. While it was characteristically functional, it was also aesthetically pleasing. The visit thereafter to the Gujarat International Finance Tec-City (GIFT City) made me wonder as to why the City had been planned so far away from Ahmedabad, and how it could hope to become a global financial centre. Little did I realize that the land itself had been selected for its non-arable nature! This way, there would be no damage to the agricultural prospects of that area. Connectivity, too, had been meticulously planned; the metro transport link, the travel time from the airport at Ahmedabad to GIFT City and the high-quality road connectivity would ensure its attractiveness. It was a telling commentary on how to build new centres of excellence which, in the course of time, would have economic multipliers.

We were supposed to go to the Statue of Unity, but all of a sudden, it was discovered that the helicopter that was to carry us might have a dicey landing in Kevadia. After consultations, the plan was abandoned. I was, however, fortunate much later to visit the Statue and realize the marvellous architectural design and its positioning, conceived and implemented by

Celebrating an Experience

Modi in record time. It was quite an experience to see both his execution skills and the facility which has been developed there.

We took a long ride to Lothal, one of the prominent sites of the Harappan Civilization. The southern city of the ancient Indus-Saraswati Civilization, Lothal, is believed to have been constructed around 2200 BCE. The city is said to have had one of the earliest known docks in the world, which connected Lothal to other Harappan cities. No wonder it was considered a thriving trade centre in ancient times, with its beads, gems and other expensive ornaments reaching the far corners of West Asia and Africa.

We also visited the Sun Temple located in Modhera village of Mehsana district. Alas, it is a rather sad version of what it originally was. We roamed around the temple, but without getting too enthused. But the visit to Rani ki Vav (literally translated 'Queen's stepwell') was far more interesting, considering that the source of water for this exquisitely crafted well came from the legendary Saraswati River, which has kindled many mythologies. We halted for a while at Patan, the home of Patola sarees, where weavers painstakingly make beautiful sarees using the double ikat technique. There are only three families in Patan that use this highly prized technique, and which only the sons of the families are taught. No matter how keen my wife, Prem Kumari, was to buy a Patola saree, the ordering and delivery time would be well into months, if not years. It also helped my wallet significantly that she finally abandoned the thought! A good Patola saree, given its exquisiteness, is, to say the least, very expensive, and expected to be an heirloom.

Those Were the Days

After Ahmedabad, we visited the city of Rajkot. My wife has connections with almost all the princely houses of Gujarat in the Rajkot area, which were like small principalities but, nonetheless, had titles. Rajkumar College has been a seat of education and learning and many of my wife's relatives secured their learning at the college.

Thereafter, the visit to the Narmada project was truly splendid. This was Modi at his best. He had taken on the audaciously daunting project of pumping water up to bring it to the parched Kutch region, and had given the area, so to say, a new avatar. Who would have imagined, hundreds of years ago, that it is possible to undertake normal agricultural operations in the water-starved region of Kutch? The prime minister had taken on this project and overseen its implementation with much precision—a quintessentially Modi characteristic.

The trip to the eastern state of Jharkhand, an area I knew very well as part of undivided Bihar, frankly, came as a bit of a disappointment. I was shocked to learn that the Ranchi-Jamshedpur highway was not operational, given difficulties in resolving contractual disputes. The project had languished for long. I could not, alas, visit Jamshedpur, a city which I love so much. Jamshedpur is an important industrial town not only because the Tata Steel plant is located there, but it is, in multiple ways, a symbol of modern urban planning in an industrial hub. I used to visit the town very frequently when I was the industrial development commissioner of undivided Bihar. I reminisced a bit about the extraordinary planning of Jamshedpur and my comfortable stay at the director's bungalow, which rivalled any five-star hotel.

Celebrating an Experience

I also recollected about Ranchi because my younger sister Radha had been the commissioner of the city. The house she occupied during her stint was the residence of the earlier regent or the commissioner to the Santhal Pargana area. It has an interesting history. The house had its own forest, hunting ground, waterfall and sanctuary; it was, indeed, a complete miniature city for the regent. It had since become the chief minister's official residence. The land has also been parcelled out for other uses; although, overall, it has been well-maintained by successive incumbents.

The dinner at the governor's residence was tastefully done and reminded me of my childhood days, when the seat of administration shifted from Patna to Ranchi, which was the summer capital. The governor now stays where the governor of erstwhile undivided Bihar stayed during the summers. I recalled the long journeys I had undertaken with my father when the headquarters shifted for the summer months. I also recalled the various tourist spots such as Hundru Falls and others, where we had spent a good bit of our childhood getting a breather from the oppressive heat of Patna. Alas, many of those dreams have been somewhat shattered by excessive urbanization, deforestation as well as political governance. We left Jharkhand with the hope that one day the area will flower again, becoming an important catalytic multiplier for India's economic development.

And now to the southern state of Tamil Nadu, which never fails to impress me, not only because of its fabled administration, but also for its old, colonial-style buildings and grand temples. I was taken aback that, notwithstanding the nationalistic fervour, the administration wanted to rejuvenate the old buildings of Lord Robert Clive and Fort St George because they constituted a part of our history, one that could not be wished away. In an era where changing names and changing history has become some kind of a popular quest, Tamil Nadu could be an example for some states. We were also impressed that in the requests for state-specific grants to the FC, the chief minister and his finance minister requested us for some resources to rejuvenate those old buildings, which had historical significance.

Our official meetings were purposive and well prepared. What particularly struck me as we were leaving, was the observation made by both Chief Minister E.K. Palaniswami, as well as Finance Minister O. Panneerselvam, that FCs may come and go but the only certainty is that Tamil Nadu's share continued to go down. I took this to heart. We have endeavoured to prove them wrong both in our interim and final report. The share of Tamil Nadu has, indeed, marginally gone up, which has hopefully reversed the legacy and the unpleasant memory harboured for long.

There are many tinsel towns but Mumbai in Maharashtra never fails to entice and attract. Its overpowering entrepreneurial energy is evident in every walk of life. For understandable reasons, the city represents the quintessential dream and quest of every Indian; the fable of rags to riches is applicable across the social spectrum. This is true not only of many young small-town actors who come to the city to become iconic Bollywood figures but also of entrepreneurs who come with very little experience or resources but end up becoming success stories. The migration of the Marwari community from Rajasthan, first to Kolkata and then to

Celebrating an Experience

Mumbai, offers many such rags-to-riches stories.

This is also true of the successful Gujarati entrepreneur community which, after the partition of Maharashtra, found new opportunities in Mumbai. Of course, there is also the Parsi community, which represents the quintessential professional class, which, notwithstanding others, effortlessly took the name depending on the profession they were in but excelled in them in multiple ways. In the legal field, the luminaries in almost every specialized branch had someone or the other from the Parsi community.

Thanks to the excellent arrangements made by the state government, we could get a darshan of the deity, Lord Ganesha, during the Ganesh Chaturthi celebrations at Lalbagh ka Badshah. There were a couple of members in our delegation who told me later that they had, in fact, experienced the power of being blessed by the deity. Maharashtra is also home to some of my favourite Indian classical music artists. Bhimsen Joshi, alas, has passed away, and so has my all-time favourite Kishori Amonkar, whom I greatly miss. Unfortunately, Pandit Jasraj, who was then alive, was not in the city during my visit. The state government did arrange an interesting evening programme of Indian classical music, but I missed the iconic classical singers who were based in Mumbai. The Indian classical music tradition in Maharashtra, of which the state has been a prime leader, along with Kolkata, needs rejuvenation. Bollywood fever, which has overtaken all other music, hopefully, can have a happier hybrid of the two genres. This will be good for the diversity of Indian musical styles as well. After all, so many famous Hindi film songs, which bring back nostalgic memories, are based on classical music ragas and its structures.

We were greatly impressed by the then chief minister Devendra Fadnavis, who had all his facts on his fingertips. He had appropriate answers to every question the Commission members had about the state's economy. He was among the few chief ministers who needed little assistance from his colleagues—either ministerial or in the civil service—to present a forceful case to the FC. He has a bright future.

Our meeting with the opposition parties in Maharashtra was more purposive than in many other states, and representatives from both the Congress and the Nationalist Congress Party demonstrated domain knowledge and experience. Maharashtra's much-talked-of administrative capabilities were in full display.

During this trip, we did not visit Pune—we had gone there earlier for a seminar arranged by the former chairman of the FC, Vijay Kelkar, with a group of noted economists. Pune represents a dominant culture as the education city of Maharashtra.

Few states can make you fall in love with them like Himachal Pradesh. The city of Shimla remains an alluring capital. We stayed at the famous Cecil Hotel owned by the Oberoi Group. It continues to be well run and meets the high standards set by Rai Bahadur Mohan Singh Oberoi, the founder who had bought the property at a nominal price from the original British owners, whom he was serving in somewhat modest formal responsibilities. While staying at the hotel, we also learned of the stories surrounding the Scandal Point. While the true sequence of events remains a mystery, the story goes that the Maharaja of Patiala had

Celebrating an Experience

eloped with the viceroy's daughter in 1892 from a place which later came to be known as Scandal Point. As a result, the Maharaja was banned from entering Shimla. He proceeded to build for himself a summer capital in the now-famous hill resort of Chail.

The old Viceregal Lodge, where the viceroy used to live, today houses the Indian Institute of Advanced Study (IIAS). The Lodge was also part of the Rashtrapati Niwas till President Sarvepalli Radhakrishnan gave it away to the IIAS, considering the little time he spent there, and the need to put this iconic building to more purposive use. I wandered around the building and, in the drawing room, came across an extraordinary collection of photographs connected with the freedom movement. Stories abound on who entered through which door, when Mahatma Gandhi left in a huff, what Mohammed Ali Jinnah said, and when Jawaharlal Nehru showed irritation and anxiety. It brought back memories of the run-up to Partition presided over by the British and the negotiations which were conducted in that very Lodge.

I was also sure that since the buildings which extensively used wood are vulnerable to unexpected fire, there had to be a well-equipped fire extinguishing system in the Lodge. We were told that all fire extinguishers were placed on top of the building, and upon further enquiry learned that they had no automatic triggers. It was assumed that when the fire downstairs gathered momentum, it would break the ceilings and the temperature being high, would automatically trigger the functioning of the sprinklers and the fire extinguishers. Quite a marvellous and thoughtful device!

The next morning, we went on a chopper ride to Jwalamukhi. We were behind schedule due to inclement weather conditions. The officials had arranged an exclusive darshan of the Jwalamukhi Shakti Peeth for us, and the visit was a humbling experience. The temple is on the Dharamshala-Shimla Road and attracts hundreds of thousands of pilgrims every year. The temple has no idol and the deity is worshipped in the form of flames which emanate from the crevices of the rock. There is a small platform in front of the temple and a mandap, where a massive brass bell hangs. No one has yet been able to figure out where the blue flames in the temple came from; and so legends abound. From there, we went to Kangra and then to Dharamshala. The drive was pleasant. It was nice to see the cricket stadium, a venture of Anurag Thakur, the former president of the Board of Control for Cricket in India (BCCI), in the picturesque background of Dharamshala. The hotel there, built by the Himachal Pradesh Cricket Association (HPCA), hosted a cultural programme arranged by the district officials. The following morning, at the Gaggal (Kangra) Airport, the plane from Delhi arrived on time and we took off.

Himachal will remain etched in my memory for its sophistication and beauty in multiple ways. Many of us had thought that the IIAS would be a good venue to write the FC's final report. Alas, this was not to be, considering the outbreak of the pandemic, which prevented any movement after the lockdown period. The final report of the Commission, much to our regret, had to be written within the confines of our homes and through consultations conducted on one virtual platform or the other.

Celebrating an Experience

THE CENTRE OF LEARNING

From Shimla, we went eastward to Bihar. It was, of course, a homecoming of sorts for me. Three things struck me. The vast changes which had taken place in the infrastructure in Patna were unbelievable. The new Patna Museum was designed by the famous Japanese architect Fumihiko Maki. It is an iconic building with a *son et lumière* (sound and light show) and displays some priceless pieces of antiquity representing the history and legacy of the Gupta dynasty. The Didarganj Yakshi of the Mauryan period is also on full display. One can only be in awe of the history and legacy of Bihar. We now have two museums: the old Patna Museum and the new Patna Museum. I remember that in the earlier days, many priceless pieces that had no space in the old museum were kept in the basement. The division of the old and new museum makes them a formidable combination. Any understanding of Indian history is incomplete without a visit to these two museums.

No trip to Patna can be complete without a visit to the private museum, known as the Quila House. It is located in the heart of old Patna and houses over 10,000 ancient artefacts, all part of famous historic tales. The Quila House was the old fort of Sher Shah and has been built at a high point overlooking the Ganga River, where visitors can see the sacred waters flowing down. It also has a well-appointed Observation Tower. One of my members greatly enjoyed the opportunity to sit for a few minutes on the original bed of Napoleon Bonaparte! We were served dinner in the original silver plates of Birbal, who was a key figure in the court of

Those Were the Days

Akbar. Having dinner in the plates of this vintage left us with a very real feel of history.

While in Bihar, one cannot miss seeing Nalanda at Rajgir. The old Nalanda University was an undisputed seat of learning in ancient Magadha from the fifth century CE to 1200 CE, when it was destroyed by Bakhtiyar Khalji. To Khalji, at the head of his advancing army, one of the monks in Nalanda said that he must contain his ego because when he is no more, he cannot occupy a land that was worth more than he measured. This may have angered Khalji, but it showed the fierce independence of the monks in Nalanda.

There is a telling story that when Xuanzang, the Chinese Buddhist monk and scholar, was leaving Nalanda to return to China, the other monks implored him to stay on and asked him why he should leave this land of learning to go to the land of the *Mleccha*—meaning foreign or barbarous peoples. To that he replied that enlightenment and knowledge should not only be confined to Nalanda, but the message of learning should be spread to other countries as well. It is fortunate that the old Nalanda University is being rebuilt, thanks to the efforts of the Bihar government and the Ministry of External Affairs on a totally new project site proximate to the site of the old Nalanda University.

One concern that strikes about Bihar is the asymmetry between its high density of population (13.12 crore) and the low availability of land. The pressure of population on land here is perhaps next only to Kerala, but it was more visible to us in Bihar. An orderly urbanization of Bihar must be a high priority. I recall that many years ago, before I became a Member of Parliament, as the deputy chairman of the Bihar

Celebrating an Experience

Planning Board, I had organized a meeting to garner private investment. One of the members was the famous Mumbai-based architect Hafeez Contractor, who, from the plane, had sketched out a new city for Patna, which would enable the pressure on the present city to be somewhat eased.

He presented those proposals to the Board, but, alas, it did not bear much fruit. The connecting stretch between Patna and Bettiah, where the new international airport is to come up, as well as the stretch on the southern side to Nalanda and Gaya, can become a perfect circular combination; in fact, it can improve on the similar project in Hyderabad first implemented by the then Chief Minister N. Chandrababu Naidu as a concept of a ring road. It could connect Patna and many of its adjacent cities and make it an important hub of change. Bihar must endeavour to attract more private investment. Currently, the absence of gainful employment opportunities makes the state the home of a substantial number of migratory labourers.

We then went to Visakhapatnam in Andhra Pradesh, via Tirupati where we had a darshan of Lord Venkateswara, arranged by the administration. From the capital, we were driven to Amaravati, the proposed new capital of Andhra Pradesh. Chandrababu Naidu was at his best, demonstrating that he could conceive and execute projects far beyond his financial resources. Never minding the debt, he believed that time and growth would pay for it. The new capital was being built on the banks of the Krishna River. He personally made sure that we saw the layout of the capital. There were separate residential complexes for the Indian Administrative Service (IAS) officers, police officers, the judiciary and the legislative.

Amaravati is perhaps the most challenging project—a new city to be constructed in post-Independence India.

While the elections were just around the corner, we did not realize at that time that given the mixed feelings, the new government, which would assume power under the young Y.S. Jagan Mohan Reddy, would want to undo the project and instead decide to go ahead for a triple capital. The successor regime to Chandrababu Naidu is not overjoyed by Amaravati and would instead like three capitals—at Visakhapatnam, Kurnool and Amaravati—for an integrated development of Andhra Pradesh and the fulfilment of old commitments. I remember with gratitude that Naidu presented me a replica of Lord Venkateswara, similar to the one he had in his office, for which I had expressed an interest.

Much later after the formation of the new government, I did return to Amaravati for a meeting with Jagan Mohan Reddy, who explained to me the economic logic of the three capitals. This would also rekindle the economy of Andhra Pradesh in multiple ways, which would mainstream the different aspirations that people in different parts of the state had from any popular government. As in the past, financial constraints and challenges would remain. It was so with Amaravati too. It would be even more daunting for three new capitals to come up.

While I wished Jagan Mohan Reddy well in his endeavour, the issue of financial sustainability of these new initiatives left me with a sense of worry. I also reflected that I was present in the Rajya Sabha during the time the Andhra Pradesh Reorganisation Act, 2014, came up. Even at that stage, I had wondered if it was economically the most sensible decision to bifurcate the state, notwithstanding the governance issues of what a large undivided Andhra Pradesh had represented. Over time, no doubt, both Telangana and Andhra Pradesh would progressively begin to realize their economic potential. Nonetheless, a remark made both by Babu and Reddy, which is perhaps one of the few points they would have agreed on, left me wondering. They both told me individually that the bifurcation was a hasty decision, that the special category benefits given by Prime Minister Manmohan Singh remained unrealized. Also, Reddy said that while Andhra Pradesh was saddled with debts and liabilities, Telangana had got away with the assets and revenues that came from that rich state. No doubt, Telangana would contest this fiercely, but the fact remains that notwithstanding the prosperity, a viable financing module for Andhra Pradesh would be a continuing challenge.

THE LAND OF GODS

Next, we visited Uttarakhand. My travel to Dehradun was a bit chequered. I seemed to have performed the unusual feat of missing my flight even though I arrived several hours before the take-off and waited patiently in the lounge. When I suddenly learned that the flight had taken off, I panicked because the programmes in the state were already fixed. However, I was pleasantly surprised to learn that several flights were lined up for Dehradun, and I took the next one in the afternoon.

Dehradun was not what it used to be when I used to transit through there on my way to Mussoorie as part of the training for IAS probationers. Being the capital now, it was congested and, notwithstanding the highways, driving through the town from the airport to the city took substantial time. The hotel I was put up in—the new Ananta Group hotel, which was nice and comfortable—was built on the foothills of Mussoorie.

I was struck by the alacrity and sincerity of the then Chief Minister Trivendra Singh Rawat, whom my granddaughter described as the chief minister of the gods because all the chota Char Dhams—Badrinath, Kedarnath, Gangotri and Yamunotri—are in Uttarakhand! I was impressed by Prakash Pant, the finance minister, who chose to give his closing address in chaste Sanskrit, though he complained that the last FC had not been just to the state.

Pant accompanied me throughout the trip. Little did I, or he, know that he had an advanced malignancy and would pass away a few months after our visit. That evening, we witnessed the Ganga Aarti at the Parmarth Niketan Ashram—it was an ennobling and satisfying experience. The next morning, we left in a chopper to visit Gangotri, which was another great feeling because this is where Bhagirathi comes down along with Alaknanda to become the Ganga. The purity of the water at Gangotri was extraordinary.

During our chopper ride, I was amazed by Pant's running commentary, recognizing every settlement and hamlet over which the flight was passing. I could then understand that 'small is indeed beautiful'. The issue of what is an appropriate model of governance depending on the size of the state came to my mind in a flash. Thereafter, we went to Nainital, a very popular summer capital in the old days but now terribly congested with hardly any good hotels. Our visit to the Naina

Celebrating an Experience

Devi Temple, another Shakti Peeth close to the Nainital Lake and about which stories abound, brought a befitting end to our visit to this beautiful state. Uttarakhand remains a small state, well managed and abounding with opportunities. The regulated, purposeful and economically efficient tourism industry has a huge scope, which regrettably has been interrupted by the pandemic. But in the post-pandemic period, this is an area to which the leadership must accord priority.

My visit to Kohima in the northeastern state of Nagaland was exhilarating. To get there, we had to first go to Dimapur and then take a chopper for landing in Kohima. We were first taken to the war cemetery in Kohima, which was quite an experience because it represented the theatre of war during the Battle of Kohima. Known to some as one of Britain's greatest battles, it was a turning point in 1944 against the Japanese U-Go offensive. The cemetery was well preserved, with the tombstone of each of the soldiers who had laid down their lives. It was also written that the Japanese had remarked, 'If we conquer Kohima, we can claim to have conquered India,' as the Kohima ridge was an important road connection for supply to British and Indian troops.

The last battle was fought in a tennis court, which was then the residence of the commissioner in Kohima. We were moved by these famous words that were prominently displayed on a plaque near the entrance to the cemetery: 'When you go home, tell them of us and say, for your tomorrow, we gave our today.' It was touching to recall that so many soldiers from India, Australia and the United Kingdom had laid down their lives to reverse the Japanese onslaught.

Those Were the Days

Chief Minister Neiphiu Rio treated us exceedingly well. It struck me that around the time of our visit, Christmas was less than a month away. And so, for the evening cultural programme, I asked the Chief Minister if we could hear some Christmas carols. He not only happily agreed, but both he and his wife sang the carols, which was most endearing. The Naga tradition of cultural vibrancy was so apparent. It also struck me when he said that the quest for a greater Nagaland had not gone out of their psyche and that they hoped to realize it one day.

This quest comprised parts of Assam and a territory within Myanmar, because the Naga community had travelled far and wide given their martial abilities. It was endearing that on the morning of our departure, the chief minister decided to take us on a short chopper ride to his village home for breakfast. It was a perfect Naga village, fenced with gates to earmark the entry and exits. The village was equipped with an amphitheatre and we enjoyed the full display of martial arts in the Naga tradition. The breakfast, which the chief minister had arranged for us, was a feast that included every conceivable Indian cuisine. Apart from the local Naga dishes, there were some in the north Mughlai style, the continental style and, believe it or not, there were also outstanding dosa, upama and idli dishes. Who says that India has not integrated effectively! If we can have masala dosa in a remote Naga village for breakfast, what more evidence is needed? The Chief Minister saw us off at the chopper ground and we took off for Manipur.

Celebrating an Experience

BREATHTAKINGLY BEAUTIFUL

For the next half an hour, we only saw mountains. Thereafter, we glimpsed lakes. Manipur is a manifestly beautiful part of India, which has many lakes and waterfronts. We were exceedingly well-treated upon arrival. Several things struck me. First, the versatile cultural talent of the Manipuri people. For the evening programme, we had a rare combination of the famous Manipuri dance and also a display of martial arts, in which the Manipuri people have achieved international excellence. The Manipuri artistic tradition, with its special style of painting, is something which will remain etched in my mind.

Chief Minister Nongthombam Biren Singh was generous enough to gift me a painting of horsemen playing games, which I continue to treasure. We recognized that Manipur had a tradition of royalty and many parts of the state displayed this in plenty. The Kangla Palace is an old mansion in Imphal which was the traditional seat of the past Meitei rulers of Manipur. With the Meitei kingdom's expansion in the 1400s, came increased conflict with the Burmese, who brought the Meitei kingdom to its end in the 1700s. I, of course, stayed as the personal guest of Governor Najma Heptulla, whom I had known for long, and was spoilt by her hospitality.

Our next stop was Odisha. I was floored by the innate simplicity of Chief Minister Naveen Patnaik. Naveen and I have been good family friends and his father, Biju Patnaik, was a friend of my late father. He invited my wife and me to a private lunch. I remember the simple menu of a soup made from vegetables plucked from his own garden, some fish and a home-made custard pudding. He offered fresh lemongrass tea and instructed his aide to cut some fresh lemongrass for us to have that refreshing feeling. We were touched by his gesture and simplicity. He was, contrary to rumours, frail, but in reasonably good health to present Odisha's case rather forcefully.

Thereafter, on our way to Puri, we visited the Sun Temple at Konark where you see the sun riding on chariots, characteristic of the sun gods and preserved so well with its vantage position next to the sea. The son et lumière that evening, especially organized for us, was enchanting. We ended our stay in Odisha with a visit to Puri and then, of course, the iconic Jagannath Temple. It is amazing how the Jagannath Temple has successfully withstood the onslaught of time, even with successive cyclones and typhoons which have devastated that region. One marvelled at this architectural wonder because nothing had happened to its structure or to its beauty over centuries even while the rest of the area has suffered destruction. I did make a commitment that the FC would like to help the lakhs of pilgrims who visit the Jagannath Temple. Looking back, I feel pleased that we have been able to provide some resolutions to improve the tourism and pilgrim facilities at the temple.

BEAUTIFUL BUT NEGLECTED

We landed in Agartala, the capital of Tripura, which had no direct connectivity—one had to go through either Kolkata or Guwahati. I felt that the Communist Party of India (Marxist) (CPI [M]), which ruled the state for 25 years, had arranged

Celebrating an Experience

to keep this beautiful state as insular as possible through poor connectivity. Left regimes have been known to avoid such developments, since issues like connectivity are not necessarily a blessing for them. When we reached Agartala, we were shocked to see little evidence of any development initiative over the last few decades. Roads, cars, houses and lifestyle seemed to have bypassed the mainstream development of India. The deliberate policy to discourage private capital was very dramatically evident. There were no hotels either. We stayed in a large guest house. All conferences were held in this very guest house and important visitors were also all housed here, which to me looked like a well-made circuit house of the old days.

Chief Minister Biplab Kumar Deb, who had taken over after the BJP had dislodged the Left, struck me as a young man with a long way to go. He is tall, handsome and almost looks like a Bollywood actor. Despite his lack of experience, he conducted the meetings with great dignity and without slipping up. I instinctively felt that something must be done to get private investment to Tripura, considering its huge untapped potential.

The visit to Tripura Sundari, which is an important Shakti Peeth, was fulfilling. The temple abounds with legends. The chief minister told me that he had been praying there just before his first election when he got important phone calls from Delhi; first, to inform him that the party was heading to a victory, and second, to ask him to get ready for an important office. He was not only a first-time chief minister but also a first-time Member of the Legislative Assembly, and he attributed it to the blessings of Ma Tripura Sundari.

We were privileged to get a darshan at the temple at a time when the pilgrim rush was low. The protocols for entering the temple were even more stringent, especially in terms of clothing, than at the temples in Tirupati or Guruvayur.

Tripura abounds with natural possibilities. Forest cover and extensive bamboo cultivation are areas which have a huge economic potential. The forest resources of Tripura and its connectivity both to Bangladesh and to other parts of India can be an important growth driver. I returned from Tripura with the conviction that something needs to be done to improve the basic infrastructure and attract private investment to boost its economy.

Now it was time to savour the famed hospitality of a north Indian state, Punjab. It fully lived up to its *mehmangiri* (hospitality). The Maharaja of Patiala and the then Chief Minister, Captain Amarinder Singh, hosted a lovely dinner, ensuring all the customs and festivities associated with the Patiala House. Finance Minister Manpreet Singh Badal, a brilliant historian who knew the inside stories of Partition in great detail, impressed me greatly with his rare collection of books on the partition of Punjab. The issue of the legacy debt of Punjab was an overarching concern and they made sure that we imbibed this message at every step.

We also spent some time with the governor of Punjab V.P. Singh Badnore, whom I had known for long, given my Rajasthan connections and the fact that both of us were in the Rajya Sabha at the same time. He used to preside over several sessions of the House and did so with great dignity. The time we spent with him at the governor's residence was truly rewarding. He was knowledgeable, generous and kind.

Celebrating an Experience

The visit to the iconic city of Amritsar provided multiple opportunities. First and foremost, we paid our obeisance at the Golden Temple on a somewhat rainy day, but did get the kind of darshan we had waited for a long time. The peace and tranquillity inside the Golden Temple will be etched in our minds for a long time. At the Golden Temple, we received a special welcome by its trustees. After an exceedingly satisfying visit to the temple, we returned to the hotel in a tranquil state of mind. Thereafter, we went to see the Partition Museum, a private initiative of a non-governmental organization (NGO) led by Kishwar Desai in the iconic old Municipal Building. It brought back the heart-rending images of what a hasty Partition had inflicted on us.

It is always a sentimental moment visiting the Jallianwala Bagh Memorial because you recall the callous cruelty of General Reginald Dyer in opening fire on innocent Indians, and why it triggered anger, revolt and revulsion even among the British. The visit to the Gobindgarh Fort for a son et lumière educated us on the history of Punjab and the valour of Sikhs in a dramatic way. It highlighted what the Sikhs had done to stave off invaders over centuries and how they fought for India's Independence as well as the extent to which they had suffered from successive ravages of war. Punjab's geopolitical uncertainties are indeed awesome and its experiences dramatic.

Carved as a separate state out of Andhra Pradesh, Telangana still has the lingering effects of the Nizam in multiple ways—its culture, food habits and etiquette. Besides, the imprint of Chandrababu Naidu, having planned Greater Hyderabad by several road linkages and ring roads as part of

Those Were the Days

his new vision, had extended to Hyderabad city in multiple ways; a classic example of improving urbanization and an outreach to other parts of the city, for which there are few recent parallels. Babu always lamented that this was his vision, but now he has to build another city. Chief Minister K. Chandrasekhar Rao (KCR), even though comparatively new in politics, seemed deeply entrenched in the new development dynamics following the partition of Andhra Pradesh.

I sat next to him for dinner and, during the conversation, he kept putting on my plate more and more varieties of Hyderabadi biryani until I was overwhelmed by not only the food but his generosity; he chose to serve it himself. Sitting right across me was Venugopal Reddy watching all this. He had been the chairman of the 14th FC and was unusually quiet that evening. One of the luncheons during our stay in Hyderabad took place at the Legislative Assembly's dining hall, which had been newly refurbished, and we were, perhaps, the first ones to receive the formal hospitality in their dining hall.

The official discussions were quite meaningful, even though at one point when one of my members kept pressing KCR on how the debt incurred for the Mission Bhagiratha project was to be paid back—namely how piped water to every home in every village (water forced through natural gravity having been pumped up) was to be ultimately repaid—he seemed irritated by the persistence. The question was a legitimate one. But at one stage, he got so offended that I feared he might walk out of the conference in protest. That would have certainly been a news item, which I certainly wanted to avoid. I deflected the discussion to the more positive aspects of the changes in the initiatives undertaken by him.

We also visited the famous Falaknuma Palace, now a Taj hotel, which was the building sold to the Nizam by his own prime minister. It was the home of his favourite Turkish wife. Falaknuma, which means 'mirror of the sky', is a towering hotel and perhaps one of India's iconic new properties. We enjoyed our afternoon high tea at the hotel. Of course, the Charminar building at the centre of Hyderabad continues to attract many tourists and provides a perfect photo opportunity. The visit to Telangana was cramped and short, but we did have useful interactive sessions with several people engaged in policymaking. Hyderabad itself has several institutions of high-quality research and our engagements with them through formal and informal interactions were educative in more ways than one.

Quite a contrast from Punjab and Telangana was Mizoram. First and foremost, under the model conduct rules in the run-up to the elections, Chief Minister Zoramthanga could not host us officially, though we were permitted to have official-level discussions. The chief minister, however, hosted a private dinner for us, which was generous of him. During the dinner, he told us a most extraordinary story. When he had filled up the form for the IAS competitive examination, he pondered for some time thereafter. He asked himself the question: if he got through, whom would he be working for? And came to conclusion that he would be working for the Government of India.

He then realized that he had another option, namely that

instead of working for India, he could work against India. He chose the latter and remained a part of the underground movement for a long time. He described to us the story of being induced by the Chinese and the Pakistani Inter-Services Intelligence (ISI) to continue his struggle, with no dearth of resources or logistics. Eventually, he joined mainstream politics and became the chief minister. On a lighter vein, a slight consequence he mentioned was that he had aged in the process and now had a young wife to look after! He did mention that he had written a book in which all these experiences were recounted in great detail.

The Mizo story is, of course, a continuing one because the Mizos inevitably ask themselves the question of whether it was worthwhile for them to give up their struggle for independence to become part of the Indian Union. There was too much calculation going on as to how much resources the Mizos were getting from the Indian government. Resources, they believed, could not be a substitute for their parting with their sovereignty to become part of the Union.

In the excellent cultural programme planned that evening, I met my very old friend Thangkima Cherpoot, who was the chargé d'affaires during my days in Tokyo. I enquired about his wife Pari, who he said was keeping very well. Thangkima looked completely unchanged from the version of what I had seen during my days in Japan. Mizos are a well-preserved lot in terms of their physical appearance and agility of mind.

There was a long gap of several months between Mizoram and our arrival at Meghalaya. The drive to Shillong from Guwahati was tiring, but Shillong remains an alluring city.

Celebrating an Experience

Chief Minister Conrad Sangma is a sophisticated person, given his excellent education in Delhi. He is the son of the well-respected politician, Purno Agitok (P.A.) Sangma, whom I had known well and who was also the Speaker of the Lok Sabha and a minister in the Union Cabinet. Purno Sangma was also one of Atal Bihari Vajpayee's favourite politicians. I knew Vajpayee's weakness for Sangma since I was, at that time, working in the Prime Minister's Office as his secretary, handling economic matters. I was in Parliament when Conrad's sister, Agatha, was a minister in the United Progressive Alliance (UPA) Cabinet. Indeed, she continues to be a Member of Parliament even now. Quite a remarkable family!

There were several highlights to our Shillong visit. This included a somewhat aborted visit which my wife undertook along with the spouses of other members of the Commission to visit Cherrapunji. She told me that it kept pouring throughout and they could hardly get a feel of what Cherrapunji was, except that it lived up to its reputation of receiving perhaps the highest rainfall anywhere in the world. We were also told of the strange phenomenon that while it rained heavily in Cherrapunji, all the water flowed back to Bangladesh. So, while we provide the rain, it is Bangladesh that reaps the benefits. Clearly, rains do not recognize or understand international borders!

In the evening, we were treated to a programme by the famous Shillong Choir. I must say it rivalled or equalled any choir group anywhere in the world. The performers were so supremely talented with their versatile range of songs and styles! At the end of the spectacular performance, I was overwhelmed by the experience and admired the style and aplomb with which the conductor had traversed and orchestrated the evening. I learned that he was also a product of St Stephen's College, of which I am an alumnus, and was a good debater of his time. I requested Conrad Sangma to thank him, but he insisted that I should do this since the choir had performed in honour of the FC. I summoned all my debating skills to try and match up to the expectations of the occasion. I was fortunate that it turned out to be one of my better speeches in recent times. Not only the conductor and the chief minister, but others too thanked me for those impromptu 'thank you' remarks!

Meghalaya also had some other interesting distractions. We visited a cherry blossom park where I realized that cherry blossoms could flourish even in India. I saw some photographs of cherry blossoms in bloom. I brought a few saplings back, but alas, the climate in Delhi proved hostile and they could not survive.

The efforts of the chief minister to not only popularize art and culture but also horticulture in Meghalaya was truly laudable, as have been his efforts to promote the local produce of Meghalaya. Agro food products will inevitably produce multiplier gains.

Going from the Northeast to the South, we were in Karnataka. We landed in Bangalore, now Bengaluru, which has several attractions. It has alluring gardens and a thriving horticulture sector. It is also an exceedingly well-planned city. It used to be a settler's paradise for long and perhaps will continue to be so in spite of it having become over-congested. I visited some of my preferred gardens, particularly

Celebrating an Experience

K.S. Gopalaswamy Iyengar & Sons, the well-known rose breeders, given my strong interest in roses. I even brought some of those roses home, which have thrived. Bangalore is widely regarded as the 'Silicon Valley of India'.

Our interaction with Nandan Nilekani, the man who helmed the Aadhaar project, and his group was exceedingly informative. We talked on the use of digital technology to improve the optimization of financial resources. The concept of direct benefit transfers of water and electricity was an important ingredient in our thinking process. The chief minister at that time, H.D. Kumaraswamy, is the son of the former prime minister H.D. Deve Gowda, under whom I had worked as revenue secretary. I visited Deve Gowda at his private home, where he was generous enough to treat me to high tea. We talked of the past, including some instances which he has also recorded in his autobiography, *Agni Divya*. Deve Gowda, contrary to popular impression, is an exceedingly intelligent man with an amazing understanding of the pulse of the people.

Notwithstanding all the other congestions, Bangalore continues to be an attraction not only for budding entrepreneurs and start-ups, but also as the Silicon Valley of India. However, the city needs rejuvenation, particularly of its water bodies. The chief minister made a strong plea that the FC deserved to give it special consideration. No doubt, the presentation made by T.V. Mohandas Pai, a titan of the information technology (IT) industry, on the need for the rejuvenation of Bangalore, made a compelling case for additional financial resources for Bangalore and, perhaps, Mysore.

The central Indian state of Madhya Pradesh had Kamal Nath as its chief minister, whom I had known for decades. He was a favourite of Sanjay Gandhi and had worked as a minister in multiple capacities. Kamal Nath is a person who can win friends and influence people with an alacrity that few can match. Whether in Delhi, Tokyo or Davos, he was a familiar face for a number of years. We were treated to his generous hospitality. We also had purposive discussions. We were struck that Shivraj Singh Chouhan, who had served as the chief minister for long, also decided to have an interaction with the FC. He did this with his usual mastery of facts and details. I realized that he viewed himself, essentially, as a chief minister-in-waiting.

After finishing our official work at Bhopal, we were taken by a special flight to Indore, once the education capital of India. Indore takes pride in once being the country's cleanest city. But what was extraordinary was the experience of the darshan at the Mahakaleshwar Temple in Ujjain. The *bhasma aarti*—an offering of ash—at the temple in the early hours of morning is an extraordinary replication of the life cycle of creation and destruction. The Shiv Ling that stands at the temple can first be seen in its plain form. Thereafter, you see it fully draped, in its glory and splendour, and within minutes, all the trappings are completely removed, and the Shiv Ling, washed and cleaned, is back in its simple elegance. Mahakaleshwar Temple is an experience in creation and destruction. In a sense, this is the essence of life—its transient nature, its growth, its creativity and then its end.

I also learned that Ujjain has a special significance in astrology. Before Greenwich became universally accepted

Celebrating an Experience

as the prime meridian in 1884, Ujjain was considered the central meridian for time in India. It is geographically located at the precise spot where the zero meridian of longitude and the Tropic of Cancer intersect. The Tropic of Cancer is significant because the latitude marks the northernmost position where the sun is situated overhead. Equally, it is also significant because it crosses the spire of the Mahakaleshwar Temple—as it does the Somnath Temple in Gujarat—and the resulting imaginary line passes through Ujjain's temple of Mangalnath. The keeping of time was considered essential to the knowledge of planetary positions, which were crucial components of forecasting auspicious days and times for the vedic rituals.

We were also lucky to visit the Omkareshwar Temple, which was a long distance away from the city of Indore. But the drive was pleasant along the Narmada River. On return, some of my colleagues also went to the street-food corner in Indore, which I was told was very popular. This street-food corner comes to life only at 9.00 p.m. and carries on till 1.00 a.m., after which, during the day, it becomes a normal bazar. The food, I'm told, is ravishing and all my colleagues who went there came back full of praise of, perhaps, the best street food they had tasted in a long time.

Chhattisgarh was the next state that we visited. Raipur is still an up-and-coming capital. I was impressed by Chief Minister Bhupesh Baghel, who exuded the confidence of an old-timer. Many people in the Cabinet of the Chhattisgarh government also looked to be seasoned political people, having worked in the Digvijay Singh government in undivided Madhya Pradesh.

The economy of Chhattisgarh, which has a large forest area with natural resources, has great potential over the coming years, but it needs concerted effort to be able to harness its potential. The chief minister is a purposive man, but would need to take more decisive action for this objective to be realized.

For me, Rajasthan, our new port of call, was a bit of a homecoming. We landed in Jodhpur, where my in-laws come from. The Umaid Bhawan was built by my wife's grandfather, partly to provide employment opportunities during a famine. Rated as one of the best hotels in India, it offers quite a magical experience. The hospitality, although technically provided by the government of Rajasthan, had all the imprint of my wife's first cousin, the Maharaja of Jodhpur. The evening programme at the palace was replete with Rajasthani traditional music; the Manganiars who sang the folk songs as well as some of the drummers had received international recognition.

The visit to Jodhpur Fort, which belongs to the ancestors of the Jodhpur family, was a nostalgic one, since I had immediately gone there after my wedding. It is also the place where my late father-in-law, the third son of Maharaja Umaid Singh, was cremated. The Thadas, as they are called in Jodhpur, are the grounds reserved for the royal family for the last rites to be performed. This tradition has been observed with a great degree of sincerity and devotion. The fort also has a temple which represents the foundation of the Jodhpur family in 1473.

After taking special permission from the Maharaja of Jodhpur, we visited this temple, which is, in some ways,

Celebrating an Experience

positioned in an overpowering way. After all, the Mehrangarh Fort has seen successive generations of the family throughout the years and this temple, therefore, has a special significance. The museum there has been exceedingly well maintained by a private trust headed by Gaj Singh, who, among the Maharaja community, is a shining example of high-quality education blended with a life devoted to the upliftment of the people of Jodhpur. I recall that, after being a member of the Rajya Sabha, he preferred to stay in Jodhpur to look after his ancestral legacy of not only property but service to the people who were the residents of the erstwhile famous Maharawal Dynasty.

From Jodhpur, we came by a special plane to Jaipur. Chief Minister Ashok Gehlot is a determined man but also with a lot of adaptability, having survived the rough and tumble of politics for decades. We stayed at the Rambagh Palace, which is also a hotel of great class, being part of the old palace of the Maharaja of Jaipur. My wife immediately recalled that, during her childhood days, she had spent a lot of time in that palace, being pampered by the Jaipur family, which had strong connections with the Jodhpur family as well.

CLOSE TO THE MOUNTAINS

Our arrival next was at Leh, the capital of Ladakh. Unlike in other places, here, we were guests of the Armed Forces. I was put up at the residence of Lieutenant General (Lt Gen.) Ranbir Singh. At the airport, I was promptly checked for my oxygen level. We were advised to take some rest in the evening since the body feels the impact of high altitude a few hours later. We rested and as expected, our oxygen level had somewhat dropped.

We visited the monastery in Leh, which has a steep climb, and thereafter rested. We slept early to be ready for a visit to Pangong Lake the following day. It was to become the geopolitical theatre between India and China. The Pangong Lake is fascinating because the colour of the water changes; you believe it when you see it. The drive to the lake was long and arduous, in spite of the experienced Army drivers detailed for us; the onslaught of snow landslides destroys the road every year. The return journey was smoother because Lt Gen. Singh gave me a ride in his chopper and we returned in under an hour, while others had to undertake the long journey by road. One has to visit Leh to realize the difficult conditions under which the Indian Armed Forces work in a terrain which is so treacherous, and with an inhospitable climate.

We found time to see a film on the Kargil War and the bravery of the Indian Army. It was a moving experience. It should be the quest of every FC to visit Leh and get a first-hand feel of what the Armed Forces encounter.

Our next stop was enchanting Sikkim. We landed at the Bagdogra Airport, and from there the drive to Gangtok along the banks of the Teesta River was long and tiring. The road was poorly maintained, particularly on the West Bengal side, which is unfortunate because there is no dearth of money with the National Highways Authority of India (NHAI). The Sikkim side of the road was in better shape, and we reached Gangtok late in the afternoon. We were received warmly. Incidentally, it is amazing how it unfailingly rains almost every evening in Gangtok! Sikkim is a totally organic state. We visited some organic farms to understand the concepts and its economics. Some members of my team also went to the Chinese border area, the Nathu La Pass. Others visited the iconic monastery in Sikkim, the Rumtek Monastery, which involved a strenuous climb, but the experience was worthwhile.

From the hills to the plains, we were in Uttar Pradesh. With its huge size and population, it is almost like a country. We began by visiting Varanasi. I was struck by three things. First, by how the city, especially its famed ghats, had been cleaned up and restored to what the original fabled Kashi was as both a religious and an educational centre. Second, by the sincerity and devotion of the district administration to improve the infrastructure. And third, by the Kashi Vishwanath Corridor. The Vishwanath Temple is almost impossible to keep clean because millions of pilgrims visit every day. Prime Minister Modi has undertaken the initiative to create the Kashi Vishwanath Corridor that will lead one directly from the Vishwanath Temple to the banks of the Ganga. We saw this for ourselves. After the special puja at the Vishwanath Temple, we witnessed the Ganga aarti, which was quite an experience. Varanasi has no dearth of temples, and we did visit some important ones, including the Sankat Mochan Hanuman Temple, and they all have many stories and mysteries surrounding them.

I was told that nearly 50 old houses were retrieved through voluntary consent because there were ancient temples around which homes had been built over the centuries. It was an extraordinary effort to bring these houses down through voluntary consent and the temples being progressively restored.

Those Were the Days

The artistic traditions of Varanasi were in full display when we visited the museum there, which shows the development of the Indian weaving and silk industry along with embroidery used on ceremonial and other occasions. No wedding can be complete without the embroider work of a Banarasi saree! I also visited Sarnath for the second time in my life, and realized the linkages between the life of Lord Buddha and the Nalanda University.

We came back to Delhi and thereafter went to Lucknow for discussions with the chief minister and his team. Uttar Pradesh represents, as I said, the size of a country, with a population of over 230 million; no wonder that its administration is a continuing challenge. We could see for ourselves the opportunities and challenges that Uttar Pradesh represents. Its administration is a well-oiled system, naturally having seen successive generations of officers with impressive domain knowledge and capabilities.

We returned to Andhra Pradesh for a second visit since the regime had changed and now had Y.S. Jagan Mohan Reddy as the new chief minister. As is customary, we began our visit from Tirupati, and after receiving darshan of Lord Venkateswara, we thereafter went by a special plane back to Vijayawada, from where we drove to Amaravati. Reddy is young and has a simple and talented wife as well. The second generation of political influence was apparent in his style. He seemed quite obsessed with the idea of three capitals instead of one. We tried to explain to him that it would be somewhat expensive to have three capitals since many states could not afford even one. He said it was embedded in the psyche of Andhra Pradesh to have

Amaravati, Vishakapatnam and Kurnool as the three capitals for the legislative, the administrative and the judiciary, respectively. We wished him luck as he grappled with multiple challenges that Andhra Pradesh encounters post the reorganization of the state.

Our final visit was to Goa, which charmed us by its informality. We were put up in an old-style hotel which had a private beach. We enjoyed the clear Goan sky, the Goan food and the cultural programme. Goans are natural singers and can burst into their cultural accomplishments at the drop of a hat. We travelled extensively in Goa. The new government under Pramod Sawant looked to be purposive. Undoubtedly, Goa has a long way to go in maximizing its opportunities as a location for international conventions, programmes, meetings and discussions. This would greatly add to the state's income and its future prosperity.

Alas, given the onslaught of the COVID-19 pandemic, which had begun to take its toll, we could not visit other states. I particularly regret that our team could not visit the Union Territory of Jammu and Kashmir. I was also not able to visit the states of Haryana and Arunachal Pradesh.

On the whole, the FC has been an amazing learning and humbling experience. The diversity of India is truly mesmerizing; its heterogeneity and homogeneity are also stupendous. The Northeast needs to be more mainstreamed and its cultural potential and skills of its people need to be optimized. They have a persistent feeling that distance alienates them from the rest of the country. This is not about money alone; it is about the mindset, which can enable deeper integration.

For example, a state like Mizoram has a population of only one million, whereas in Bihar, Patna alone has a population of over two million, and as a whole, Bihar has a population of over 124 million. The sheer difference in scale, size and complexities makes it difficult to comprehend how we have kept ourselves together. Expectations from the FC also remain high. Our state travels were federalism in practice—with all its innate challenges and opportunities.

Long live the FC as a balancing wheel of our federal polity!

◆

N.K. Singh was the chairman of the 15th FC.

FULFILLING CHERISHED DREAMS

New Family, New Friends

Prem Kumari

I was lucky to accompany my husband, who was the chairman of the 15th FC, on quite a few of his state visits. For me, it was not the assignment but the fulfilment of a personal quest to see places of religious, cultural and social significance in different parts of the country. I subsequently succeeded in realizing that dream.

The 15th FC, I found to my delight, is like a close-knit family. The spouses were also bound together and were my companions during the journeys.

My dream began in Assam with a visit to the Kamakhya Temple. I had gone there many times earlier and had always made a promise to return. The power of the deity reverberates in my mind and heart; I know that she does not allow her devotees to go back with a feeling of emptiness. The visit to the Assamese silk and cultural centres lived up to my expectations of Assam's great legacy. The cultural recital was also very interesting. I had never seen a performance in which mother and daughter performed equally well—it was difficult to say who was better.

Kerala, too, had many attractions. I had never been to the Sree Padmanabhaswamy Temple in Thiruvananthapuram, even though my sister-in-law's husband was a governor there. The visit to the Guruvayur Temple, among others, was equally exhilarating. The Metro ride in Kochi was a novel experience. I never realized that even in non-metro cities, the Metro could be so effective in meeting mass transportation needs.

West Bengal was quite an experience and I thoroughly enjoyed every moment of that visit. After all, how can one overlook the special sandesh and rosogollas in Kolkata? This is notwithstanding the unsettled controversy of whether rosogollas come from Odisha or Bengal. I was also delighted to visit Kali Mataji's Temple while in Kolkata.

Gujarat taught me a lot, as I travelled with my husband in parts of Kutch, Ahmedabad and Lothal. Many of my relatives had small principalities there: in Limbdi and Dhrangadhra, to mention a few. I recalled with fondness the time I had spent at the Baroda Palace with my aunt, who was married to Fatehsinghrao Gaekwad.

Maharashtra had its own high point for me. I had been to Mumbai several times but had never realized that it was so difficult to get a proper darshan of the Lalbagh ka Badshah, which I was privileged to see.

Himachal Pradesh has its multiple charms. In Shimla, I

Fulfilling Cherished Dreams

learnt about the Scandal Point, which my younger daughter Madhavi was quite curious about. Having a darshan at Jwalamukhi was exciting. Therein lies a cold blue flame which has been there for hundreds of years. Nobody knows where it comes from. Unusual, right? When we crossed Kangra on our way to Dharamshala, I realized that I had many relatives there, particularly my first cousin who had married into the Lambagaon family. My daughter's in-laws also come from Kangra, a really beautiful part of the country.

Bihar was a homecoming for me. I had seen it all but thoroughly enjoyed a revisit to the Jalan Museum. I could not conceal a bit of laughter when many of the members got a kick out of sitting on Napoleon's bed and enjoying their food in fine cutlery.

Andhra Pradesh always has the attraction of a visit to Tirumala. I had always wondered how the temple's management kept the place so clean, with thousands of people eating there every day. If we can have a clean city with so many pilgrims in Tirumala, why can't we do the same for the rest of the country?

Uttarakhand had every conceivable package for me—for example, visits to Gangotri, Kedarnath and the Naina Devi Shakti Peeth in Nainital. Could I have asked for more? I was also delighted to meet Naveen Patnaik in Bhubaneswar. We had known each other for long and he was affectionate in remembering his relationship with my first cousin, the Maharaja of Jodhpur. His simplicity was overpowering.

In Tripura, visiting Tripura Sundari was a great experience. I had always dreamt of visiting Tripura Sundari, and could not believe that this quest, too, had been realized.

Those Were the Days

In Punjab, it was a great pleasure to meet the then Chief Minister Amarinder Singh again, who is related to the Jodhpur family since his aunt had been married to my father's elder brother. He was really warm and affectionate. My visit to the Golden Temple, with its peaceful and serene ambience, was an overpowering experience.

I remember Mizoram and Meghalaya for the vibrant cultural experience. In Shillong, along with the ladies' group, I ventured out to see Cherrapunji. I had hoped that it would not rain but as we stepped out, we were completely drenched within seconds. The drive back to Shillong to change into dry clothes was memorable, though miserable.

In Bangalore, it was a feast for me because I visited all the nurseries. I might mention that apart from visiting the temples, I equally enjoyed visiting nurseries everywhere I went. I collected pots and plants, little realizing that not many of those plants would be able to withstand the extreme temperatures of Delhi.

The visit to Rajasthan, my home state, began from Jodhpur, where I was born. Meeting all my relatives again and being pampered as a daughter of the family as well as in my new capacity as the wife of the chairman of the FC, was both nostalgic and fun. The Umaid Bhawan Palace was my wedding venue, in 1967. I realized that it looked the same as I remembered. Many of my relatives are gone now, but it filled me with nostalgia. I also had an opportunity to have a darshan of Chamunda Mata at the fort, and thereafter, visit the place where my father was cremated. It was touching.

Varanasi is always overpowering. My last visit to the Kashi Vishwanath Temple was several years ago. Manoeuvring

Fulfilling Cherished Dreams

through the narrow lanes of Varanasi, whether on foot or by other means of transport, was a daunting challenge. Issues of hygiene and sanitation had always been problematic. I was, therefore, quite pleasantly surprised to find the city cleaned up. We had a perfect darshan of Lord Vishwanath and subsequently also got to watch the Ganga Aarti on the banks of the Ganges.

Manipur and Nagaland are contrasts with one thing in common: culture, which is very much a part of life in both the states. Culture not only in terms of performance but also habits, style, mindset and the traditions of the original artisans. Manipuri paintings are really quite extraordinary. What a talented set of people!

I realized the foolish mistake I made by not going to Hyderabad. My husband had fallen ill in Hyderabad and was alone and miserable there.

It all ended happily, though, in Goa, with the cool and pleasant feeling of walking along the beach.

On the whole, I thoroughly enjoyed being the wife of the chairman of the FC. I knew it would be only for a short while, but no happiness lasts forever. It did enable me to realize the great dream I had of seeing the temples of India, across the length and breadth of the country, in comfort and style.

Long live the FC! Long live the spouses who have become my friends for life.

◆

Prem Kumari accompanied her husband, N.K. Singh, on some of his trips.

SOME INCREDIBLE JOURNEYS

We Will Remember Them All

Anoop Singh

What I would like to do is go to the other side of being part of the 15th FC. By 'other', I mean beyond the many pages of the four volumes of our report. I will share a few of the memories from my time in an institution that I realize is an indispensable part of India's federalism—memories of times when I could also briefly escape from the intensity of the state visits.

I had expected this to be an interesting job, but I had not expected it to be quite so incredible. Visiting nearly every state and meeting the regional leaders of modern India as well as the people, with their myriad cultures and their hidden talents which we are yet to discover, made this

Some Incredible Journeys

assignment a collage of sentiments and beauty that blew my mind.

How is one to explain this? The diversity of India vastly transcends that of any other country I have visited. As the lockdowns were gradually relaxed, many in our country started planning trips abroad, rather than in India. We all need to rethink and instead appreciate the people and talents in different parts of India which are making the country, slowly but surely, a much-sought-after destination. India is very big and, therefore, it is no wonder that our state visits were too many to recall here. I will not talk about the places you know well (say, the Golden Temple in Amritsar or the Venkateswara Temple in Tirupati), but focus more on the somewhat hidden parts of India's natural beauty and talents.

THE NEW RAIPUR, THE OLD ARUNACHAL

Let me start with Naya Raipur in Chhattisgarh and then move on to the North and the East. Naya Raipur is a planned city, India's sixth, with a dedicated safari area. It might not be among our most well-planned cities or the most popular safari, but it is definitely new, green and upcoming. There is more to see in the habitats of its jungle safari, one of the largest of its kind in Asia, than you might imagine. And you will definitely see tigers as I did, and much more. When in Naya Raipur, you will notice the attention it is giving to climate change by keeping more than a quarter of its land for afforestation and greenery.

Now to Arunachal Pradesh, as far north and east as you can go in India. The state is a hidden treasure, with its arts and dances, languages and tribes and subtribes, whose numbers exceed that of many states. The evening dance show that we had the good fortune of seeing looked stunning against the twilight sky. And to my pleasant surprise, they all speak (and sing) in Hindi better than me! Their rituals and fertility dances remain an essential part of their sociocultural heritage. They can be devotional as well as symbolic of events of everyday life. The dances need to be understood better, as they convey how myth and folklore combine with the rituals of today. Visit Arunachal Pradesh for its song and dance and its celebration of life.

The weather kept us from paying a visit to Tawang, but we splashed in the turbulent and uncontrolled Lohit River, which originates in eastern Tibet and then merges with the Brahmaputra River. We saw its caves that attract many devotees and display the histories of times past. The many pilgrimages to Arunachal Pradesh, from different cultures and beliefs, centre around the Lohit. Its banks are a treasure house of medicinal plants and herbs, and also home to Mishmi tita (the Coptis teeta plant), known for its medicinal properties.

GLOBAL TREKKERS' PARADISE

Then we visited Ladakh, the home of global trekkers, where we stayed with the Indian Army. We travelled to Pangong Tso Lake, which is at an altitude of approximately 14,000 feet above sea level, through the highest motorable mountain pass in the world. The colours of the blue-and-green Pangong Lake, and of the Himalayan mountains around it, defy description.

Some Incredible Journeys

As evening descends on Leh, Zorawar Fort tells you, through its spectacular sound and light shows, the history of the place, including the victory over the Chinese. There is more to Leh than I can recount here. The monasteries in Leh can beat the ones in Bhutan. The pashmina shawls available in Old Leh Road is a must-buy. Make sure you stay at Dragon Hotel while visiting Leh. Then we saw the rest of India's Northeast, with its vibrant culture.

HISTORY IN A NUTSHELL

Let's make Nagaland the focus point of my recollections in the Northeast. Special mention must be made here of the grandeur and solemnity of the Kohima War Cemetery, which recalls the role India played in the Second World War and the Nagaland State Museum, which exhibits ancient weaponry, ceremonial drums and cultural artefacts. The state is home to a large number of wild orchid species. We were treated to Nagaland Coffee in a delightful café outside our hotel. When I asked as to why coffee from Nagaland was not competing with Starbucks, I was told that the process of bringing about awareness and competition is underway. We were particularly taken aback by the hospitality of the people during an early morning festival, where the entire village had come out to celebrate— led by the chief minister, who was warm and welcoming. Make no mistake, the region has immense potential, though commitment and finances are needed to bring about the much-needed headway in infrastructure. Well, I could go on, but I will stop with the state of Himachal Pradesh, parts of which are called the 'Switzerland of India'.

Those Were the Days

THE LAND OF SNOW

First, let us talk about Dharamshala, the home of His Holiness the Dalai Lama (whom, alas, we did not meet), and the Tibetan government-in-exile. We met the local bodies, as we always did during our trips elsewhere too. I learnt about their accomplishments in health and education. The talent of the young was in full display at an art fair, where we all acquired works of art by budding artists. I discovered a wonderful bookshop-café called Illiterati, which serves organic delicacies made from fresh local produce. The wood stove and outdoor seating make for a great ambiance. Barnes & Noble have come and gone in many parts of the world, but Illiterati remains.

And then there is Shimla, the summer capital of British India, with its incredible architecture, much of it centred around the famous Mall Road. And now, in Shimla, let me end these quick memories with a personal recollection. Amazingly, for the first time, at the top of the mall I stumbled into a park and saw the monument built in memory of my uncle, an army general who died the year after the 1962 China war, as it happened tragically, on the same day as John F. Kennedy's assassination.

Well, these are some of my fondest memories from my official trips. I will perhaps not get the opportunities and challenges of the same intensity and the enjoyment of getting to know the many parts of a country as varied and diverse as India. The exhilaration of working with an outstanding team cannot be forgotten. Life has to go on and I will hold onto these beautiful memories.

Some Incredible Journeys

The context is clearly different, however I cannot help but recall the words of Captain Amarinder Singh, who once cited English poet and dramatist Robert Laurence Binyon (from his poem 'For the Fallen'):

At the going down of the sun and in the morning,
We will remember them.

◆

Anoop Singh was a member of the 15th FC.

JOY, HOPE AND NOSTALGIA

Overawed by Diversity

Ajay Narayan Jha

When I was told, while still serving as finance secretary in the middle of preparations for the interim Budget 2019-20, that I was being appointed as a member of the 15th FC, I was in a dilemma. Having served the earlier FC as secretary, I wondered whether I could bring anything new to the table this time, wedged as I would be with the architecture, thrust and direction of their recommendations. Yet, there was a feeling of challenge that I saw in the Terms of Reference of this FC, which were sharply different from those of the past.

There are several attractions of being part of an FC. The job requires a detailed study of each state from the fiscal perspective, supplemented by a visit. Where else do you get to visit all the 28 states of our great, diverse nation? During such visits, you get opportunities to meet and interact with the political leadership, the bureaucracy, the representatives of local bodies, the media and, on field trips, sections of the general public. However, it is the cultural dimension that remains etched—a necklace with each stone so different from the other but joined together by the cord of unity, of which the FC is one significant thread.

The camaraderie and bonding that develop between the Commission members and the staff as the FC travels from one state to another is much deeper and abiding than what working in the Secretariat and formal meetings achieve. Discussions, exchange of notes and even gossip over meals and morning walks break barriers and take you beyond the written words and data that come in abundance on a variety of issues. Little nuggets and nuances, which otherwise get overlooked, emerge out of casual interactions with the accompanying officers who are very junior in hierarchy but who work intensively in their domain. I have felt that I, as a member, have learnt more from my junior colleagues than, perhaps, what they may have gained from me.

I carry with me many memories of my journey with the 15th FC, but some are precious and unforgettable. The trip to Khecheopalri Lake, northwest of Pelling town in Sikkim, was one such. The decision to visit emerged from the evocative description of the place by fellow member, Ashok K. Lahiri. So we decided to make a detour via Pelling on the day before the Commission's visit to Sikkim. Driving from Bagdogra through West Sikkim, we reached Khecheopalri just as the sun was going down—the light sufficient enough to capture the ethereal beauty, splendour and sublime charm of the water body.

THE SACRED LAKE

The Khecheopalri Lake is sacred for both Buddhists and Hindus, and is believed to be a wish-fulfilling lake. The local name for the lake is Sho Dzo Sho, which means 'Oh Lady, Sit Here'. It is ensconced in the midst of the Khecheopalri hill, a sacred spot and a land of hidden treasures blessed by Guru Padmasambhava. Although we did not have the time to venture to the hilltop, the lake looks like a giant footprint, associated with Goddess Tara and Lord Shiva. An interesting feature of the lake is that leaves are not allowed to float in it. It was fascinating to watch birds industriously pick them up as soon as they dropped onto the lake's surface. A footbridge lined with sacred wheels, took us over a marshy swamp to the edge of the lake. As we stood there throwing *moori* (parched rice) for fish to come and devour, each of us made our wish.

As the monsoon had not ended, it was raining intermittently. I set the alarm for sunrise, not sure if I could catch a glimpse of Kanchenjunga with clouds playing spoilsport. But the weather smiled! As sunrays filtered through the sky, there it was in all its majesty and splendour. First, the little orange tinge and then the glowing yellow as the sun gradually rose in the eastern sky. For half an hour, I stood there mesmerized, sipping endless cups of Temi tea and absorbing the natural beauty in silence and reflection.

As you travel from state to state, you get to savour the distinct and unique cuisine of each state. Guwahati is not just an entry point for the Northeast, it is the confluence of diverse cultures and cuisines of the ethnic groups inhabiting both the state of Assam and the region. Our stopover for a night at Guwahati en route to Shillong took some of us

Joy, Hope and Nostalgia

fish lovers to Maihang Ethnic Restaurant, in the heart of the city. The sheer variety—10 different types of fish cooked in 10 different ways—with each tickling the palette with its distinct taste. But then, the surprise was the professional art of serving. Just as the desire rose to have more of a dish, the next one would emerge from the kitchen! For a foodie like me, it was an experience like none before.

But more importantly, I left with a surge of pride because the Northeast had changed since I had first set foot there 37 years ago. One of the ways to judge this, arguably, is by the standard of hotels and eateries because they reflect the ease of travel and pleasure in which tourism can thrive. The quality of food, ambience, service and professional conduct matched the best in the country and left me convinced of the immense potential waiting to be tapped.

Often, we talk about a 'bucket list' of things to do and places to visit. For me, a journey along the Narmada—'Narmada Pradakshina/Parikrama' from Amarkantak to the Arabian Sea across the heart of India—is one such adventure that I have always wanted to embark upon. Ironically, till our state visit to Madhya Pradesh took us to Indore, I had never seen the sacred river. Some of us drove down to Omkareshwar, one of the 12 *jyotirlingas* (radiant signs of the Almighty), and then onward in incessant rain to Maheshwar. Maheshwar is known for its spiritual importance, the great Holkar Queen, Rani Ahilyabai and the famous Maheshwari handloom sarees and fabric. The town has several buildings and public works that Rani Ahilyabai Holkar got constructed in the eighteenth century. The pièce de résistance is the majestic fort with the riverfront ghat, strikingly similar to the ghats of Varanasi. The resemblance in layout, design of the ramparts and the steps are almost a replica of Varanasi. No wonder, a number of movies get shot in Maheshwar! Despite the drizzle, we ventured out to the riverbank, with Narmada in full spate. The devout amongst us stepped into the river to take the *anjali* (offering and blessings). As Adi Shankaracharya wrote in 'Narmadashtakam':

> *Sa-Bindu-Sindhu-Suskhalat-Tarangga-Bhangga-Ran.*
> *jitam*
> *Dvissatsu Paapa-Jaata-Jaata-Kaari-Vaari-Samyutam |*
> *Krtaanta-Duuta-Kaala-Bhuuta-Bhiiti-Haari-Varma-De*
> *Tvadiiya-Paada-Pangkajam Namaami Devi Narmade ||1||*

(Salutations to Devi Narmada)! Your river-body
illumined with sacred drops of water, flows with
mischievous playfulness, bending with waves;
Your sacred water has the divine power to transform
those who are prone to hatred, the hatred born of sins,
You put an end to the fear of the messenger of Death
by giving Your protective armour (of refuge); O Devi
Narmada, I bow down to Your Lotus Feet. Please give
me Your Refuge.

The majestic sight and the exquisite beauty of the river took my breath away. At least, a part of the bucket list got fulfilled. The remaining journey from Amarkantak will await another day.

How could we visit Maheshwar and not go shopping? We first went to a store run by a trust which manages an NGO that organizes weavers, supplies yarn, provides guidance

Joy, Hope and Nostalgia

in latest fashion trends and also offers financial, marketing and sales support. However, the main market typically was a street full of shops on either side. The sheer variety and range of fabrics and sarees is overwhelming as is narrowing down the choice and final selection especially for someone like me who was not accompanied by my wife. But thanks to WhatsApp and its video feature, there was a continuous dialogue and display of choices with the wife, and the selection made. Maybe when I do the Narmada Parikrama, I will bring her along to Maheshwar.

My visit to Raipur was equally interesting. I first visited the city when Chhattisgarh had just become a state, and for the next few years, my job required me to go there very often. Raipur was at best a district headquarter town, far from being the capital city of the state. The one standard hotel, Hotel Babylon, stood host to all visiting officers. With the previous FC I had visited and seen the settlement of Naya Raipur, the new capital complex, coming up. Babylon Hotel still remained the preferred place to stay. Now, on this recent trip, the growth and development that have marked the state over the last two decades are very visible. Amongst other things, Babylon Hotel has grown into Hotel Babylon International, a huge complex, like a five-star property!

However, the most impressive was Naya Raipur, the beautifully planned city catering not only to the expanded government but also the large number of people who now inhabit Raipur. The city has been planned keeping in view the needs of the future in terms of connectivity and technological advancement, without compromising on ecological balance and conservation. The best example is the Nandanvan Jungle

Safari, skirting Naya Raipur, where wild animals are kept in earmarked enclosures akin to natural surroundings but spread over large areas.

NORTHEAST DELIGHT

If Naya Raipur took me by surprise, Kohima in the Northeast won my heart. As you enter Kohima town from the helipad on the Imphal-Kohima National Highway (NH) 39, one of the most prominent landmarks is the War Cemetery commemorating the soldiers who sacrificed their lives in the Second World War. It is maintained by the Commonwealth War Graves Commission. On the slopes of Garrison Hill is what was once the deputy commissioner's tennis court. This tennis court was also the scene of the one of the fiercest fighting between the Allied army and the Japanese forces.

The poignancy of seeing the names of soldiers, some as young as 17 years and hailing from all parts of the British empire, including India, as you go around the cemetery, is heart-wrenching. For me, having served in neighbouring Manipur, thinking of several thousands of our own Indian lives lost in the protracted insurgency that afflicted the states of Nagaland and Manipur for decades, the sadness was even more deep.

But as you proceed to Kohima town, the change in Nagaland becomes visible. You can see the benefits of investment and economic development in the form of infrastructure (barring the NH, which was being repaired), connectivity and prosperity. To have a feel of rural Nagaland, we took a trip to Khonoma, an Angami Naga village, about

Joy, Hope and Nostalgia

20 kilometres west of Kohima. The village resisted the British for almost 50 years before calling a truce in 1879. This was also the village of Angami Zaphu Phizo, who started the movement for a separate Naga nation around India's Independence, and later in the 1950s became the architect of the Naga insurgency. But today, Khonoma prides itself as India's first 'green village'. Decades ago, it had completely stopped *jhum* (slash-and-burn cultivation) and shifted to terrace cultivation. Now, the hunting of wildlife and birds is prohibited and a part of the village forest is dedicated to preserving wildlife. We also discovered that the village has set standards in conflict-resolution mechanism and development-oriented village administration, something that is now being emulated by other villages in the state.

As I left Kohima, en route to Dimapur and Delhi, I saw the double-lane work of NH 39, the famous highway along which tales of war and insurgency are woven in the region. I hope the work and the accompanying development as part of India's Look East policy now weave tales of peace and brotherhood.

It feels odd writing these lines, living as we do now in a state of social distancing, face masks, video conferences and restrictions on travelling and intermingling. For me, as memories of the last 18 months come flooding back in kaleidoscopic flashes, I just hope that normalcy returns soon and we start ticking our individual bucket lists from this great, diverse country.

◆

Ajay Narayan Jha was a member of the 15th FC.

BETTER LATE THAN NEVER

Many Beautiful Moments

Ranjana Jha

I was a late-comer into the 15th FC family. But not for a moment did I feel as if I had not known them for years. A small WhatsApp group of spouses added to the bonding and sharing of our joys and I felt very welcomed from day one. Tales from the travels across the country made me both excited and eager to visit places that I had not gone to before. However, at the time when my husband joined, the general elections were on and no travel to a state could take place.

So when the trip to Karnataka came along post elections, I joined Ajay (Narayan Jha). I had been to Bengaluru on a short visit for a family wedding. But then, it was what you call a point-to-point trip. The first port of call, Mysuru, provided the first glimpse into the history and magnificence of the culture, heritage, architecture and arts of Karnataka. The grand Mysuru Palace, its meticulously curated museum, the surrounding gardens and the sound and light show simply enthral you. The following morning began with a trip to the Chamundeshwari Hills and a darshan of the Devi.

Having grown up on Bollywood songs filmed at the famous Vrindavan Gardens, I was eagerly waiting for a trip there. I must admit though that it was a bit disappointing as the upkeep was wanting. Something I did not miss during the drive around the city was its remarkable cleanliness. I was told Mysuru ranks very high in the Swachh Survekshan (cleanliness survey) index. The City Corporation needs to be complimented for its efforts.

No visit to Mysuru is complete without a trip to Srirangapatna, the capital of Tipu Sultan's empire. The Dariya Daulat Palace (Summer Palace) is set amidst beautiful gardens called Daria Daulat Bagh. Built in 1784 by Tipu Sultan, the palace is made of teak wood, has a rectangular plan and is built on a raised platform. What captivated me most, apart from the impeccable architecture and layout were the beautifully manicured gardens. Tipu Sultan's Fort is surrounded by double walls and an obelisk marks the point at which the British broke through the walls, and surprised Tipu Sultan's troops. The town is famous for an ancient temple dedicated to Sri Ranganathaswamy, another avatar of Lord Vishnu. Several other temples dot the town. But for the limited time available, I could have easily spent the whole day seeping in the rich religious and political history of the place.

The ride back to Bengaluru can become excruciating with heavy traffic building up as you approach the city. But once you reach the city, it offers tremendous opportunities for shopping, relishing the varied cuisine of the region and leisure walks in Cubbon Park. With the rest of the group, we had a glimpse of important landmarks in the city, interspersed with visits to Cauvery (the state emporium) for sandalwood agarbattis and incense and the standard shops and simply gallivanting at Brigade Road-MG Road. The coffee in the India Coffee House on MG Road is absolutely superb and can give the best amongst the new coffee chains in town a run for money.

A visit to Ladakh was something we all were looking forward to. I can never forget that trip! The day prior to the journey I kept sniggering at Ajay for the multiple antidotes he was taking in order to beat the side effects of high-altitude sickness. I refused to take any, insisting that I was fighting fit. So I was, when we landed. An hour into our arrival, I felt slightly light-headed. I thought it would pass after the customary rest that we were all advised. Lo and behold, by lunch time I was slowly sinking, with a sudden drop in my oxygen level. By evening, it had worsened enough for me to be rushed to the military hospital and put on a drip! I have little memory of that night except that glint in Ajay's eyes saying, 'See I told you that antidotes are needed!' Sadly, I missed the visit to the famous Pangong Tso Lake, and even more sorry for having made Ajay miss it. The bucket list remains unfulfilled.

However, we could make up a bit with local sightseeing in Leh, a visit to the fabulous War Museum followed by a superb sound and light show, roaming around the shopping boulevard and savouring the local cuisine of momos and thukpas with fresh trout grilled to perfection using local herbs. Our local host advised us to see the morning women's market in Leh. A number of women vendors were selling local fruits and vegetables: fresh bok choy, broccoli, lettuce and fresh and dried peaches. It reminded me somewhat of the famous Women's Market, Ema Market, of Imphal!

Unfortunately, I could not join Ajay and the rest of the group for a few other state visits. I wish I had.

◆

Ranjana Jha accompanied her husband Ajay Narayan Jha on some of his official visits.

A COUNTRY LIKE NO OTHER

Recording the Learning

Ashok K. Lahiri

After my appointment as a member of the 15th FC, Arun Jaitley, the former Union minister for finance, gave me a piece of advice. 'Carry a notebook, and write down your experiences in the various states,' he had said. So, I did, and now I realize how valuable that advice was.

Nothing pleases me more than when I can visit remote parts of my country and experience for myself the true meaning of unity in diversity that is India. Anyone who does not know the diversity, does not know India. At the same time, anyone who only knows the diversity without comprehending the unity in diversity in the different parts of India, has a very imperfect and faulty understanding of the country. Many of the British colonial rulers, for example, Sir John Strachey and Sir Winston Churchill, perhaps wistfully,

A Country Like No Other

saw only the diversity and didn't see the wood for the trees.

Sir John Strachey was a distinguished member of the Bengal Civil Service who acted as the Viceroy after the assassination of Lord Mayo (Richard Bourke, 6th Earl of Mayo) in 1872. In 1888, in his book, *India...*, he said he could never imagine Punjab and Madras (now Chennai) as parts of a single political entity.[*] Four decades later, in 1931, Sir Winston Churchill said: 'India is no more a political personality than Europe. India is a geographical term. It is no more a united nation than the Equator.'

Nobel laureate Amartya Sen refers to Emperor Akbar's vision of India, which acknowledged India's internal diversity as early as the sixteenth century. He notes, 'The extent of that diversity has baffled many. Indeed, many centuries later, when Winston Churchill made the momentous announcement that India was no more a country than was the Equator, it was evident that his intellectual imagination was severely strained by the difficulty of seeing how so much diversity could fit into the conception of one country.'[**]

Many colonialists would raise their eyebrows at the idea of an independent India. Our founding fathers, Mahatma Gandhi, Pandit Jawaharlal Nehru, Sardar Vallabhbhai Patel and Bhimrao Ramji (Babasaheb) Ambedkar, among others, recognized both the diversity as well as unity as 'something deeper and within its fold.'[***] In our Constitution, they gave us a quasi-federal structure, which combines the advantages

---

[*]John Strachey, *India...*, Nabu Press, 2012.
[**]Amartya Sen, *The Argumentative Indian*, Penguin, London, 2005, p. 39.
[***]Jawaharlal Nehru, *Discovery of India*, Oxford University Press, Delhi, 1989, p. 62.

of being a big country with those of being a small country. The federal structure, along with the reorganization of states in response to popular demands based on language or cultural subtleties, has stood us well. We do not have to go far to see its usefulness. The example of Pakistan, India's twin separated at birth, serves us well.

Pakistan, formed in 1947, had two wings (one on the west and one in the east), separated not only geographically by about 2,000 kilometres of Indian territory, but also in terms of language and culture. While East Pakistan had mainly Bengalis, West Pakistan had a bewildering diversity with Punjabis, Sindhis, Balochis and a few others. The stitching together of East and West Pakistan was similar to the temporary amalgamation of Spain and much of the Netherlands in the second half of the sixteenth century under Philip II of the Habsburgs, the King of Spain. Around the same time, as India was securing its federal structure by reorganizing the states in the mid-1950s, Pakistan, under General Sahibzada Iskander Ali Mirza, first as its interior minister and then as its president, was moving in the opposite direction.

Mirza, from East Pakistan, had a distinguished lineage from Nawab Syed Mir Jafar Ali Khan Bahadur, better known as Mir Jafar, who was the general of Siraj-ud-Daulah, the last independent Nawab of Bengal. In 1757, at the Battle of Plassey, Mir Jafar betrayed Siraj's trust, defected to Robert Clive of the East India Company, laid the foundation of the British empire in India and thereby became the Nawab of Bengal, as a puppet of the Company. If Mir Jafar destroyed the independent kingdom of Bengal, almost two centuries later, in 1955, Iskander Mirza sowed the seeds of Pakistan's destruction by moving the Bill for its 'One Unit' policy. He went on to become the first president of Pakistan on 23 March 1956, and acquire the distinction of abrogating the Constitution of Pakistan on 7 October 1956 and declaring martial law.

Under the 'One Unit' policy of 1955, Pakistan would be one unit with no Bengalis, no Punjabis, no Sindhis, no Pathans, no Balochis, no Bahawalpuris and no Khairpuris; only Pakistanis. This was expected to strengthen its integrity. The policy failed in less than a decade and a half. Its reversal became a critical necessity. In 1970, President Yahya Khan created the four provinces of Balochistan, the North-West Frontier Province (NWFP), Punjab and Sindh in West Pakistan. And, instead of there being no Bengalis and only Pakistanis in East Pakistan, in December 1971, East Pakistan itself became the new independent state of Bangladesh.

With the separation of Bangladesh, the new Pakistan in 1971 was what the poet-philosopher Muhammad Iqbal, as president of the Muslim League, in 1930 had wanted: an independent Muslim state consisting of Sindh, Balochistan, Punjab and the NWFP. While Pakistan means 'land of the pure,' Choudhary Rahmat Ali, a young student studying at Cambridge in England, coined the term 'Pakistan' in a pamphlet *Now or Never* in 1933, as an acronym for **P**unjab, **A**fghania (the NWFP), **K**ashmir and **I**ndus-Sind, combined with the '*-stan*' suffix from Balochistan. Rahmat Ali's Pakistan never included Bengal or Bangladesh in Pakistan.

While Pakistan pursued its One Unit policy, India continued creating new provinces. After Andhra Pradesh in 1956, Gujarat and Maharashtra in 1960, Nagaland followed in 1963, Haryana in 1966 and Himachal Pradesh in 1971. On 3 September 1970, the Government of India announced in Parliament that it had decided, in principle, to grant statehood to Manipur and Tripura. Later, similar announcements were made in respect of the autonomous state of Meghalaya, and the separation of the Mizo District and the North-East Frontier Agency from the state of Assam, which became Union Territories and were known as Mizoram and Arunachal Pradesh, respectively. By 1972, the number of Indian states had gone up from 14 to 21. With the creation of the new states of Sikkim in 1975, Arunachal Pradesh, Goa and Mizoram in 1987, Chhattisgarh, Jharkhand and Uttarakhand in 2000 and Telengana in 2014, the number of states reached a high of 29 in 2014. The FCs owe a special debt of gratitude to the federal structure enshrined in the Constitution: they exist because of the federal structure of the Indian Republic.

Even before joining the 15th FC, I was lucky to have been to all the states except Arunachal Pradesh, Chhattisgarh, Mizoram and Nagaland. But it was never enough. Every time I visited a state, I learnt something new. I had the privilege of knowing several of the chairmen and members of the previous FCs and had some idea of the nature of work and the extensive touring involved. Both the work and the visits turned out to be more challenging and exhilarating than what I had ever imagined.

THE CIVILIZATIONAL DEPTH

My tales from the 15th FC can fill up a whole book. For brevity, let me thus focus instead on a few highlights and start with the way it all began, with a visit to Arunachal Pradesh. Who does not know about Arunachal Pradesh, where the Tawang Monastery, the second-largest Buddhist monastery in the world after Potala Palace in Tibet, is, right? The authorities wanted us to pay a visit to the monastery, but because of inclement weather we could not. Instead, we went to Namsai, which in sharp contrast to Tawang in the northwest, is near the eastern corner of Arunachal. In Namsai, the visit to Kongmu Kham or the Golden Pagoda, with its serene atmosphere and spectacular 45-feet-high gilded bamboo statue of the Buddha was a lifetime experience. Thereafter, we took a two-hour road trip through picturesque, undulating green hills to Parashuram Kund, which is on the Brahmaputra plateau in the lower reaches of the Lohit River and 21 kilometres north of Tezu in the Lohit district.

Legend has it that Lord Parashuram, the sixth incarnation of the Hindu god Vishnu, was guilty of killing his mother Renuka under the instructions of his father Rishi Jamadagni. Parashuram beseeched his father and got his mother restored to life, but the *kuthar* or *parasu* (battle axe) with which he had committed the matricide would just not come off his hand. He travelled from place to place and did penance, and finally it came off only after a dip at the Parashuram Kund. The trek to the kund, the view of the fast-flowing blue Lohit and a dip in the kund made the trip a memorable one. Hopefully, the dip also washed away all my sins!

I am always amazed at the Chinese government's claim on Arunachal as South Tibet. I have often wondered whether the Chinese government also claims that Parashuram was a Han Chinese or it granted him a tourist visa to travel to the kund!

Those Were the Days

Let me skip a couple of state visits and jump to Kerala, which had a special significance because of its stellar achievement in areas such as education and health, and its backwaters and coastline. The Finance Minister Thomas Isaac is an economist, who taught the subject at the Centre for Development Studies at Thiruvananthapuram until the mid-1990s. As you all know, we economists are very liberated souls. Yet, let me confess that, as a fellow member of the guild, I had an extra dose of comfort with Thomas's presence in Kerala.

We were staying at a hotel in Kovalam where the waves of the Arabian Sea lapped the building just below our balcony. Far away from Arunachal, again I was reminded of the legend of Lord Parashuram. According to legend, Parashuram, after exterminating a whole lot of warrior kings because of their wayward behaviour, in a mood for renunciation, donated all his conquered land and treasure to Rishi Kashyap, who ordered him to leave the land. Parashuram wandered to the Western Ghats and asked the Lord of the Seas to recede to make space for him. The Lord of the Seas asked him to throw his axe to demarcate the border to which he wanted the sea to recede. Parashuram did that and up came the land mass of Kerala and the Konkan Coast, which are still known as God's Own Country and Parashuram Kshetra, respectively. Looking at the blue waves of the sea in the southern tip of the country and recalling Parashuram Kund in Arunachal, I marvelled at the large distances across the country that some of our illustrious ancestors traversed before the advent of maps, roads, motorized vehicles, trains, aeroplanes and the GPS.

When we go to buy mangoes, we ask for Langra, Dasheri, Chaunsa, Hapus, Neelam or Amrapali. We do not ask the shopkeeper for rice, but for Basmati, Parmal, Gobindobhog or Sona Masoori. The country has several varieties of bananas, and often I have wondered why we cannot get a variety of them in shops. Kerala is well known for the different types of bananas available there and I asked one of the officials accompanying me if I could get a sample of the variety. I am glad I did. Within a couple of hours, I had six different types: Robusta, Kappa Vazha or Chenkadali, Kadali or Rasakadali, Palayamthodan and Poovan. My fervent hope is that, even if not in my lifetime, in big Indian cities, at least my grandchildren will be able to ask for Rasakadali or Poovan rather than just bananas!

THE BALANCING ACT

Working with the FC, you learn about the importance of maintaining interregional balance in the country. So, let me narrate glimpses of our trip to Gujarat in the west, where the authorities took us to Patan, a very old town in the northern part of the state. We went to Rani ki Vav or Ran ki Vav (the Queen's stepwell), by the banks of the now-lost old Saraswati river. It was constructed during the rule of the Chalukya or Solanki dynasty by Queen Udayamati in memory of her deceased husband. The architecture resembling an inverted temple divided into seven levels of stairs with sculptural panels depicting religious, mythological and secular imagery was a unique experience. Looking at it, I thought the country has got so much in terms of tourism potential!

The bonus in Patan was a visit to Sahastraling Talav/ Talao (the Tank with a Thousand Shivlings), near Rani ki Vav. There, I also found the mausoleum of Bairam Khan, the commander-in-chief of the Mughal Army and the guardian, mentor and regent of Emperor Akbar. Khan was born in Badakhshan (now in present-day Afghanistan), in the high Pamir plateau, which I had the privilege of travelling to. In fact, I was quite surprised to find his statue in Tajikistan, where he is revered as a hero.

In the very first year after Akbar's father Emperor Humayun's death, Hem Chandra Vikramaditya, also known as Hemu, a Hindu, had threatened Mughal rule by capturing Agra Fort and defeating the Mughals in the Battle of Delhi in October 1556. Almost a month later, in November, at the Second Battle of Panipat, Bairam Khan was instrumental in defeating Hemu, beheading him and securing the Mughal rule. What I find fascinating about Bairam Khan's story is his loyalty to the Mughal royal family and the natural impatience of Akbar, still in his teens, not to have a regent anymore! In 1560, Bairam was banished to go to Mecca, and on the way, near Sahastraling Talav, was killed by Haji Khan Mewati, a Pathan General in Hemu's army, to avenge his master Hemu's death. A Pathan Muslim in a Hindu king's army killing Bairam to avenge a defeat and beheading is yet another story about the unity in diversity that is India! That is what makes the Mausoleum of Bairam Khan in Patan worth a visit.

Let me now turn to our visit to Tamil Nadu and its capital Chennai. I had been to Chennai many times before and to Fort St George, which houses the legislative building and other offices of the government of Tamil Nadu. I knew a

A Country Like No Other

bit about Fort St George's almost 400-year-old history, but never had the occasion to visit the historic landmarks and the monument and learn about the Fort's important role in history. Fortunately, S. Krishnan, a former colleague in the Ministry of Finance, Government of India, was the additional chief secretary (finance) in Tamil Nadu. In between official meetings, Krishnan volunteered to take me to the museum and St Mary's Church.

Fort St George, named after the patron saint of England, is where, in 1744, Robert Clive, the controversial builder of the British Indian empire, started his career in the East India Company as a 'writer' or an ordinary clerk. Born in a minor feudal family, Clive was a very unruly and violent boy right from his childhood days. Apparently, in the beginning of his career, the unfriendly and quarrelsome Clive was so miserable and lonely that he attempted suicide twice in Fort St George. The pistol misfired both times. After two failed attempts, many believe that Clive decided that destiny had reserved something better for him and refrained from further attempts at suicide. Of course, that is only until his successful endeavour much later in November 1774 after his return to England. In Bengal, from our childhood, we were familiar with how, in the Battle of Plassey in 1757, Clive had defeated Siraj-ud-Daulah, the last independent Nawab of Bengal, by bribing Mir Jafar, the commander-in-chief of the Nawab's army. We as children had often wondered what would have happened if Clive had succeeded in his attempts at suicide at Fort St George!

Fort St George also houses St Mary's Church, the oldest Anglican church in the country. St Mary's Church was a special attraction for me because this was the place where the wedding of not only Robert Clive with his wife Margaret Maskelyne but also of Elihu Yale with Catherine Hynmers was consecrated. If Clive is known for his role in setting up Britain's Indian empire, Elihu Yale is famous for his generous contribution in founding the Yale College, which later became the world-famous Yale University in New Haven, Connecticut, in the United States. Yale is named after Eliha Yale and has produced such outstanding economists as William Vickrey, Edmund Phelps, Paul Krugman and George Akerlof.

Elihu Yale was a British-American merchant, who was born in Boston and grew up in Britain. He served the East India Company for two decades and became the first president of Fort St George in 1687, more than half a century before Clive's arrival in India. Both Elihu Yale and his ways of acquiring fortune are controversial to say the least. But we can take solace from the fact that whatever, if any, that was plundered from our country contributed to the setting up of the Yale University.

We will recall that Sir John Strachey, the distinguished member of the Bengal Civil Service, in 1888, had said that he could never imagine Punjab and Madras as parts of a single political entity. So, let me conclude my brief account of tales from the FC by recounting our trip to Punjab in the north. I wondered what Sir John would have to say in his grave about the FC visiting both Tamil Nadu (erstwhile Madras) and Punjab to decide on fiscal devolution! Or, for that matter, about the leading Sikh families of Tamil Nadu running the Guru Nanak College in Chennai for almost half a century!

A Country Like No Other

Chandigarh, one of the new cities that independent India built, never fails to excite me. In Chandigarh, what was striking was a visit to the house of Pierre Jeanneret, a Swiss architect, who in collaboration with his cousin Le Corbusier, designed and built the city. I did not know that Le Corbusier was the pseudonym of Pierre's cousin Charles-Édouard Jeanneret! The pictures in the house, which is now a museum, gives a fairly good idea of how enormous the project of building Chandigarh was!

We were also lucky that the Punjab authorities took us to Amritsar, from where we could go to Wagah border and also have a much-cherished darshan of Harmandir Sahib or the Golden Temple. First, we went to Wagah, at the border with Pakistan. Wagah, on the historic Grand Trunk Road, is only 24 kilometres from Lahore and 32 kilometres from Amritsar. Lakhs of hapless refugees had crossed over at this border during the dark days of Partition.

At Wagah, at sunset, we could watch the famous and colourful lowering of the flag ceremony, when the Indian Border Security Force (BSF) and the Pakistan Rangers parade and lower their respective national flags. The boisterous parade with legs raised to unbelievable heights looks like a choreographed piece and filled spectators on both sides with national pride. It rained while the parade was going on and I am happy to report that none of us, including the young ladies in our team, moved an inch until the flags were lowered. The BSF were kind enough to offer us some hot pakoras and tea before we left for our hotel. We changed our clothes and went straight to the Golden Temple. The meticulous cleanliness of the shrine, the soulful kirtans (narrations) and the sacred atmosphere made it a memorable experience.

When the darshan got over, it was dinner time. We headed for Makhan Restaurant at Majithia Street. Coming from West Bengal, I know a thing or two about fish. But never could I imagine fish fillet in batter deep-fried in butter! Reluctantly, for the sake of full disclosure of the truth, I have to give credit to Punjabi cuisine that it does make a mouth-watering dish.

I could go on about our equally exciting visits to other states, but then there will be no space left for my other colleagues to write. So, let me end with a word about how and why, in writing its report and formulating its recommendations, the trips were important for at least me, if not the whole FC.

Policies must reflect political realities, social mores and popular aspirations across states. The same policies are unlikely to work for both Burkina Faso and Belgium. The trips enlarged my understanding of the Indian diversity as well as the unity in that diversity. What I have done is narrate only a few tales from the trips. Translating into words what I imbibed in terms of the subtle diversity in culture and not-so-subtle differences in the political economy or needs of the states would require an entire volume. Hopefully, the reader will find some of what the FC found in this regard described in the Report of the 15th FC of November 2020.

◆

Ashok K. Lahiri was a member of the 15th FC.

AN OPPORTUNITY OF A LIFETIME

Costumes Tell a Story

Rita Lahiri

When Ashok (Lahiri) gave me the news that he was going to be part of the 15th FC, he immediately added, 'We will be visiting all the states of India, and you can come along for all the trips.' I was thrilled to think that I could see places that I had always wanted to see! I decided that I wanted to celebrate this once-in-a-lifetime travel experience by commemorating one of India's most diverse and celebrated art forms: its textiles. I would buy at least one saree from each state I visit, so that I would have a lasting record of the special creative arts of each Indian state.

We started with Arunachal Pradesh, which was particularly exciting as I have always been keen to learn more about the northeastern states. We reached Itanagar by helicopter and stayed as the guest of the governor. On the first day, we were given a tour of the city by two ladies who gave us immense insight into the culture and customs of the people there. We visited the Donyi-Polo (Sun-Moon) Temple, which was a very simple structure with a simply adorned altar. The followers are animists, an ancient indigenous religion. Then we visited the monasteries of the two sects of Buddhism—Mahayana and Theravada, which are followed by many people in the state.

Our visit to the local museum was very enlightening. I learnt that there were 26 tribes living in Arunachal Pradesh, each with its own language. Because of this wonderful linguistic variety within a single state, the common language they use is Hindi. Each tribe could be identified by its dress; for example, the handloom skirts the ladies wore. The Galo tribe wore white and black, the Adi wore red. I really enjoyed tasting the local food and watching the dances of the different tribes. I came back thinking that we know so little about the Northeastern states of India.

My next trip was to Kerala: I thus went from the hills of Northeastern India to the emerald-green seashore of southern India. We landed in Thiruvananthapuram, on my birthday, and it was just before the onset of the monsoon. We stayed at a beautiful seaside hotel, and the waters were wild, with huge waves crashing just below the window of my room. I spent a lot of time just sitting in the balcony watching the sea and the tall coconut trees swaying to the wind. It was one of my best birthdays! We were four of us on this trip: Prem Kumari, Lopamudra Das, Gita Mehta and

An Opportunity of a Lifetime

me. All of them were so friendly and warm that soon we were having a wonderful time together. We were treated to a lovely traditional dinner, with foods like appam, vegetable stew and avial, among many more dishes. We also watched a marvellous Kathakali performance.

I had never been to Madhya Pradesh, so I was very excited to go to Bhopal. I had heard so much about that place and the lake there. Bhopal is a lovely town and from there we made a trip to see the Sanchi Stupa and the Bhimbetka caves. I was particularly impressed with the Madhya Pradesh Tribal Museum, where I could step inside full-sized models of the tribes' houses and dwellings and feel as if I had been transported to a village where they live. From Bhopal we went to Indore and then to Ujjain. On the way back from Ujjain to Indore, some of us travelled via Maheshwar, which was the capital of the kingdom ruled by Rani Ahilyabai Holkar in the late eighteenth century. Her palace on the banks of the Narmada River is small and beautiful. Rani Ahilyabai started the tradition of Maheshwari saree weaving, with its distinctive warp and weft being silk and cotton, which makes it lightweight and slightly glossy, and I ended up buying quite a few unique ones.

Our visit to Leh, in Ladakh was a memorable one. I stepped out of the aeroplane and was amazed by the stark beauty of the majestic mountains. Our visit to Pangong Tso or Pangong Lake was a unique experience. We went on very rough roads, and some of us, including me, had a tough time with the high altitude and motion sickness. But I am very happy and grateful that I got a chance to see the stunningly beautiful lake. Blue waters of the lake with brown mountains at the back: nothing green could be seen in that extraordinary landscape. It was breathtaking!

A few days after Ladakh, we took our trip to Sikkim. I loved every minute of the long drive from the Bagdogra Airport to Gangtok. The road runs along the river Teesta. There was lush green vegetation on both sides of the road and also a few small waterfalls. It was a kind of mountainous beauty that was the exact opposite of Ladakh. In Gangtok, we visited the famous and impressive Rumtek Monastery, which is the seat of the Karmapa Lama or the head of the Karma Kagyu sect of Tibetan Buddhism. Seeing scores of playful young boys being trained as future Lamas was a memorable sight.

In Ahmedabad (Gujarat), we visited the Sabarmati Ashram of Mahatma Gandhi, which is such a peaceful place situated by the river. On the way to Gandhinagar from Ahmedabad, we stopped at the Gujarat International Finance Tec-City (GIFT City), where we spent half a day learning how new Indian cities might look in the future. After this trip to the imagined future, we delved deep into the past, on a visit to the archaeological remains of a Harappa Port town at Lothal. This was very inspiring for me, for I had read about Lothal in the newspapers and had long wanted to visit this place built by our ancestors thousands of years ago. From Gujarat, a state which is famous for Kutch embroidery and tie and dye, I bought a beautiful tie-and-dye, locally called Bandhej, saree.

We spent a couple of days in Jaipur before heading back to Delhi. The town of Sanganer, which is about an hour's drive from Jaipur, is famous for block printing on cloth. We

An Opportunity of a Lifetime

ladies spent a day visiting the factories and learning how the blocks were cut on wood and then used for printing sarees and other materials. We enjoyed wonderful Rajasthani cuisine and the hauntingly beautiful folk songs at a reception that was organized for the FC. And yes, I did buy a saree from Jaipur, a Lehariya saree, which can be recognized by its diagonal tie-and-dye pattern.

In Chennai, Tamil Nadu, we visited the famous church where St Thomas, one of the 12 apostles of Jesus, was buried. This church was built in the sixteenth century by the Portuguese, and later renovated by the British. In Rameshwaram, we visited the wonderful Ramanathaswamy Temple, with its huge pillars and ornate corridors. We drove to the end of the island just in time to see the breathtaking sunset, and crossed the famous Pamban Rail Bridge on the way. Tamil Nadu is famous for Kanchipuram sarees, and I loved examining the Kanchipuram silks in bright, vibrant colours with their intricate zari pallus and borders.

I was not, in the end, able to visit all 28 states, and I have not been able, in this short piece, to describe all the wonderful places that I did visit. I have such wonderful memories of the then Nizam's collection at the Salar Jung Museum in Hyderabad, in Telangana; a boat ride with Prem Kumari in Vijayawada and a visit to Amaravati in Andhra Pradesh; and the early morning Ganga Aarti on the ghats of the Ganga River in Varanasi. I will never forget the Jagannath Temple in Puri, which I always wanted to visit, and our visit to the Chilika bird sanctuary, with its glorious abundance of unique and colourful birds.

Our last trip was to Goa. Anita Bajar, Gita Mehta, Prem

Those Were the Days

Kumari, Nirmala Kota and I frolicked like teenagers in the waves of Candolim beach. It was so much fun!

I have collected many sarees in the last two years, and every time I look at them, all my memories of the places I was fortunate enough to visit come rushing back. I feel blessed to have been able to see so much of our extraordinarily diverse and complex country, and to have brought a small part of each state's artistic accomplishments back home with me.

◆

Rita Lahiri accompanied her husband Ashok K. Lahiri on some of his official visits.

Top: Chairman, N.K. Singh (third from left) and members of the 15th Finance Commission meet representatives of the Autonomous Councils of Assam in April 2018 in Guwahati, Assam. Ashok Lahiri and Shaktikanta Das are standing first and second from the left, respectively.

Bottom: An enthralling evening cultural show 'Many Journeys, One Dream: The Arunachal Story' being performed at the Arunachal Pradesh Legislative Assembly Hall, Itanagar in April 2018.

Top: Chairman and members at the Guruvayur Temple in Kerala, in June 2018. N.K. Singh is second from right.
Bottom: Working women impress with their self-reliance during a visit to Self-Help Groups at Kemia Khamarpara Gram Panchayat, West Bengal, in July 2018.

Top: Chairman and members of the Finance Commission visit the Gandhi Ashram at Sabarmati in Gujarat in July 2018.
Bottom: Chairman of the 15th Finance Commission, N.K. Singh, being briefed during a visit to Lothal, an ancient port town during the Harappan Civilization in Gujarat, in July 2018.

Top: Chairman and members enjoy a cultural performance at the evening programme in Jharkhand in August 2018.
Bottom: Glimpses of a visit to the Dr A.P.J. Abdul Kalam National Memorial at Peikarumbu in Rameswaram, Tamil Nadu, in September 2018.

Chairman and members with representatives of major political parties, trade and industry and local bodies in Mumbai, Maharashtra, in September 2018.

Chairman and members of the 15th Finance Commission at the Viceregal Lodge, also known as Rashtrapati Niwas, in Himachal Pradesh in September 2018.

Shaktikanta Das sits on a replica of the throne of King Ashoka in the Patna Museum, Bihar in October 2018.

Chairman and members seek the blessings of Lord Balaji at Tirupati, Andhra Pradesh, in October 2018.

Top: Shaktikanta Das and N.K. Singh with a dancer on the banks of River Krishna, Andhra Pradesh in October 2018.
Bottom: A cultural dance programme at the home town of the Chief Minister of Nagaland Neiphiu Rio in the Touphema Tourist Village in November 2018.

Top: An evening cultural programme in Imphal, Manipur, in November 2018.
Bottom: Chairman of the 15th Finance Commission, N.K. Singh, visits the Kohima War Cemetery in Nagaland in November 2018.

Chairman N.K. Singh poses next to a sand sculpture by the world-renowned artist Sudarsan Pattnaik in Puri, Odisha, in January 2019.

Top: Dancers enthral the audience at the evening cultural show in Tripura, in January 2019.
Bottom: N.K. Singh at the Golden Temple (Sri Harmandir Sahib) in Amritsar, Punjab, in February 2019.

Top: Chairman and members interact with the Chief Minister of Telangana K. Chandrashekar Rao and other representatives of the state government in Telangana in February 2019.
Bottom: A cultural dance show at an evening dinner programme in Aizawl, Mizoram, in March 2019.

Top: An evening with the Shillong Chamber Choir in Meghalaya, in June 2019.

Bottom: Chairman N.K. Singh (third from the left) and member Ashok Lahiri (second from right) pose with the other members and their spouses on the banks of the Narmada River in Madhya Pradesh in July 2019.

Dr Dileep Makhija at the double-storeyed Buddha in the Thiksey Monastery in Leh, Ladakh, in September 2019.

Chairman of the 15th Finance Commission N.K. Singh (fourth from left) meets Dr Pramod Sawant (third from left), the chief minister of Goa, in Panaji, in January 2020.

UNDERSTANDING CENTRE-STATE TIES

Federalism at Work

Ramesh Chand

My visits to various states were a unique and memorable experience in several respects. Besides understanding the economy, finance and fiscal health of the states, these visits apprised us of the initiatives being taken for socio-economic transformation and the overall development of each state by the current and recent state governments. The interactions with chief ministers and their Cabinet colleagues, representatives of third tier, industry and the media equipped us with state specificities and how they can contribute to cooperative federalism. Field visits in each of the states provided us wonderful and enriching occasions to understand the culture and see historical sites and monuments. Cultural programmes organized by the states were the best medium to understand the diversity and richness of India's heritage.

The visits started from the easternmost part of the country, i.e., Arunachal Pradesh. Its cultural affinity with the rest of the country needs to be seen to be believed. The hydropower project of Arunachal Pradesh is a great initiative to meet the power demand of a big country like India. The cultural programmes in the Northeastern states were mesmerizing and provided an insight into their music and folk culture.

The interaction in Haryana provided insight into reforms in rural local bodies and the wonderful role these institutions were playing in cleanliness, hygiene, sanitation and beautification of rural habitations.

Kerala is known for participatory development. This can be seen from the involvement of local NGOs in food supply for the Integrated Child Development Services (ICDS) Scheme and management of rural schools.

States have very high aspirations as India is catching up with global economic powers. This was visible in the initiative like Mission Bhagiratha in Telangana. There, the state has undertaken a very ambitious initiative for the supply of drinking water to each household and to spread irrigation by lifting water from the Krishna and Godavari rivers and their tributaries up to the Deccan plateau.

Another example of this aspiration was seen in Ahmedabad, where the GIFT City is coming up as the International Financial Services Centre. The state also offers impressive example of Smart City projects.

Understanding Centre-State Ties

The state of Rajasthan impressed us with its hospitality. The Commission visited a water-harvest site near Jodhpur, and it was a coincidence that nature brought a very heavy shower—something rare in that region—when we were having a big get-together with the farmers and rural people in the countryside.

Madhya Pradesh has emerged as the best-performing state in the country in agriculture, with double-digit growth over a long period of time. Hundreds of people visiting the Mahakaleshwar Temple, as early as 4.00 a.m., bore testimony to the faith of numerous Indians in ancient spiritualism.

The visit to the state of Uttar Pradesh convinced us that this is a land of artisans, craftsmen and also artists. The state has a great chance of promoting One District One Product and combining it with the revival of micro, small and medium enterprises (MSMEs).

How bountiful and beautiful nature can be was best experienced during the visit to Uttarakhand and Himachal Pradesh. A visit to Gangotri and the horticulture sites show the immense potential for economic development of the states through spiritual tourism, horticultural development and ecotourism. We also tasted very delicious apples produced in the Harsil valley. But apples in Harsil are still produced in small quantities and not many people know about them. Despite immense potential, horticulture and floriculture in Uttarakhand are restricted to limited pockets.

Neighbouring Himachal Pradesh, despite a low level of industrial and service activities, is ranked much higher in per-capita income and other socio-economic outcomes such as health. The state has some of the best sites in the world for nature lovers. One such site near Shimla is the Shimla Water Catchment Wildlife Sanctuary, in Seog. You are really in the lap of Mother Nature when you are inside this sanctuary. The state can earn immense revenue by developing tourist infrastructure such as cottages and other amenities in appropriate places.

Punjab is known for its warmth and remarkable hospitality, which we experienced at its best during our visit. The state finance minister accompanied the Commission throughout, especially on a field visit and to the Holy Golden Temple. This will remain a memorable part of 15th FC's visits.

The visit to Leh was organized by the Army brass and we were taken to Pangong Tso Lake and the frontier pickets neighbouring China. Kudos to the brave hearts who protect our frontier. They live in extremely inhospitable terrain and climate. The nation can never repay the debt it owes to them. In our visits to some Buddhist shrines near Leh, we experienced the serenity and spirituality of these sacred places.

◆

Ramesh Chand was a member of the 15th FC.

A BOUQUET OF SWEET THOUGHTS

Savouring Enlightening Moments

Anita Bajar

It was a matter of great pride for me to join my husband, Ramesh Chand, in some of the state visits of the 15th FC. Due to my professional commitments, I could visit only a few states such as Uttarakhand, Himachal Pradesh, Uttar Pradesh, Madhya Pradesh, Odisha, Karnataka, Rajasthan, Goa and the Union Territory of Ladakh. These visits provided me unique experiences in every field. Learning about the culture of various states and visiting important places with Madam Prem Kumari, Ms Rita Lahiri, Ms Lopamudra Das, Ms Geeta Bhatia, Ms Nirmala Ravi Kota and Ms Chetna Bhatia made it all the more interesting. We became good friends, spent time together during these visits and soon became like a family.

Those Were the Days

Seeing the puja at Gangotri, visiting the Ganga Ghats in Varanasi and seeing Mahakaleshwar and Jagannath Puri, with excellent arrangements made by the states, was like a dream come true.

Great shopping experiences in the company of liaison officers helped us in selecting the best produce of various states. On several occasions, we bought many things on the spur of the moment.

The experience of flying in the helicopter with Mrs and Mr Shaktikanta Das, RBI governor, over the picturesque snow-clad Himalayas to Gangotri Hills, always remains fresh in my mind. It was indeed a mesmerizing experience.

Meeting the chief ministers of all the states and tasting the ethnic food served in the special dinners can never be forgotten.

Visits to historic monuments in the states and exploration with the assistance of experienced guides were enriching for both the eyes and the mind.

The visit to Leh as a guest of the Army reminded me of my childhood days spent in Army culture. The pain and care taken by senior-level officials to look after our comfort spoke of the respect shown to women in Army culture. My heart goes out to those brave hearts who live in such an inhospitable environment, where even breathing was a challenge for us. Their sacrifice for our safety and national integrity cannot be expressed in words. I salute them.

The biggest gain of these state visits is the closeness I have developed with Madam Prem Kumari and Shri N.K. Singh and their daughters, Madhavi and Meenakshi. The memories of these visits will always remain fresh in the beautiful

A Bouquet of Sweet Thoughts

pictures I clicked with the help of Mr and Mrs Ravi Kota.

♦

Anita Bajar accompanied her husband, Ramesh Chand, on some of his trips.

AN INSTITUTION THAT BREATHES

Working in Tandem

Arvind Mehta

It is 9 November 2020. I sit at my desk on the twenty-first floor of our Janpath office, gazing out at the Tricolour fluttering atop its majestic flagpole at Central Park, Rajiv Chowk. We had just returned from the Rashtrapati Bhavan, after having submitted our report to the president of India—for the next five years (2021-26). Our constitutional mandate is now complete. I silently salute our beloved National Flag.

Flashback to 12 October 2017. On my daughter Radhika's birthday, I join the Ministry of Finance situated in North Block. My immediate task is to set up the office and Secretariat for the 15th FC. Which does not yet exist. No office, no staff, no records, no advance cell—nothing. This

An Institution That Breathes

vacuum will always test the mettle of a Secretary designate! I start my talent search process. Some recruits are the diamonds who have already withstood the heat of previous FC experiences. Some are roughs who I picked—in whom I can see the potential sparkle!

The 15th FC was formally notified on 27 November 2017. As secretary to this Commission, I meet the chairman designate N.K. Singh. He tells me that he and the members would be formally joining in the first week of December. I inform him of all the steps already taken to get the required posts sanctioned and recruitment process already done for the Commission staff.

I also inform the chairman of the sanctions obtained and lease agreement signed to hire the office premises in Janpath. The contract with the architect firm to design the office spaces as per our requirements were signed. Action already taken to make our Commission green—through hiring of electric vehicles and setting up of charging stations at our new office premises.

Meanwhile, through some *jugaad* (work-around), the consultative process with various stakeholders is immediately started. As I soon learn, the chairman is numero uno in consulting a wide spectrum of stakeholders and domain experts!

We start the shifting-in process of our officers into the brand-new office spaces at the end of January 2018. Able and enthusiastic officers set up the required systems for interconnecting our ninth, twenty-first and twenty-second floors, through state-of-the-art intercoms, internet, telephones and fax lines, computers, office furniture and fixtures. Our swanky new conference room (named after Kshitish Chandra Neogy, the chairman of the 1st FC) is in place. It overlooked the breathtaking landscape of Rajpath, India Gate, Parliament and the offices of the most important ministries of the Government of India from the lofty heights of our twenty-second floor.

We start our states' consultative process with Arunachal Pradesh as our first state on 5 April 2018. The chairman and I agreed that it would be symbolically significant to start with Arunachal. It will perhaps take an entire book to record all the impressions and education we gained from our visits to all 28 states, as also to the Union Territory of Ladakh. I will attempt just a few very salient thoughts and leave the rest to my fellow authors of this anthology.

Our travels confirmed economic history: the East India Company (and subsequently the British Raj) bequeathed a legacy of poverty to South Asia. There is yet much work to be done if we are to catch up with the rest of the world.

The eastern parts of India, notably east Uttar Pradesh, Bihar, Jharkhand, Assam and West Bengal, are suffering an exacerbated brunt of historical legacies, which need amelioration. While the strategies for anti-poverty programmes for each of these states will require a more nuanced approach, some broad personal thoughts may be worth recording here.

The floods emanating from the rivers of the Himalayas in these regions wreak great annual damage, especially for the people of Assam and Bihar. Such disasters impede farming and other incentives for economic activity, making it difficult for the inhabitants to break out of their cycles of recurrent flood damages and consequential poverty. Major

An Institution That Breathes

capital and afforestation works are essential for integrated upstream river basins' management. However, these cannot be accommodated through FC awards since the gestation lags of such river basin management projects would stretch over 10-15 years. National priority projects are urgently required for such river basins. Only such holistic upstream projects can properly address poverty issues in these areas, through proper flood mitigation. A piecemeal downstream approach will simply witness yearly washing away of river embankments.

Arunachal Pradesh has great economic potential. It is very sparsely populated, even in the vast areas of its river valleys. A greater density of its population in these areas will surely spur economic activity. Some innovative thought will need to be given by the state government to allow greater leasing of land for both farm and non-farm economic activities.

As we moved from state to state, we witnessed how much the state governments are trying to achieve in their developmental process: from drinking water, irrigation, health, education, sanitation, waste-to-energy, roads, optical fiber connectivity, renewable energy, to tourism and related connectivity—the list is endless! We hear the same refrain: how many of their dreams of progress collide against the harsh reality of paucity of financial resources.

We travelled to Leh to take a briefing from the Armed Forces of their international border management issues in the area on 15 September 2019. We steeped ourselves in the history of Leh: how it came under the domain of the Indian civilization, emanating from the Army conquests of the Dogra kings of Kashmir. We drive right up to the Pangong Lake, which borders Tibet, to familiarize ourselves with the defence preparedness issues of this region. The discussions are prescient, as the events in this area unfolded in 2020.

In Leh, the Indus River, which gave birth to the Sindhu river civilization, is indeed majestic. The Buddhist monasteries in the area are awe-inspiring as they overlook the Sindhu River from great heights. Nirvana!

We had reserved the large state of India, Uttar Pradesh, for the very end of our travels. With a population of more than 200 million, it merits attention as among the largest states in the country.

We travel to the holy city of Varanasi on 20 October 2019, the city that is famed for providing *moksh* to all souls that come for liberation at the ghats of Ma Ganga.

We had gone to Varanasi primarily to familiarize ourselves with the steps being taken by the state government to clean up the holy river through better sewage treatment plants and other such measures. I spent some time understanding from my escort officer how the dust pollution of Varanasi could be better managed by leaving no dirt cracks between the metaled roads and the side pavements. A lesson worth emulating for all other cities of India.

At Varanasi, the Buddhist relics of Sarnath left a deep impression on my mind. They resonate with our earlier trip to Nalanda in Bihar. There is a compassion that permeates their history and this can only be felt and not described.

Early next morning, I take a swim in the pool of our hotel. The feeling of Buddha's compassion takes over again as I do my silent laps and meditation. Suddenly, this compassion speaks to me urgently: why are so many of India's children still hungry and malnutritioned?

An Institution That Breathes

This question makes me ponder as to what we can do about this issue through the FC. The next day, in our meeting with the Uttar Pradesh chief minister, Yogi Adityanath, we exhort him to ensure that the state starts doing better than the national average in child nutrition. If we want India's social indicators to improve, it is imperative that the state starts performing better than the country average.

I leave Uttar Pradesh convinced that if India is serious about its human capital and demographic dividend, the country has to ensure that nutrition of lactating mothers and infants is given the highest priority.

In this anthology, my wife Gita asks the question: 'Where do I begin?' My dilemma is: where do I end?

Of all that we learned and observed in our FC, there are so many thoughts that swirl in my mind. We travelled together as a family, creating happy memories. These I leave to my spouse to record, as she is truly my better half.

I am sure that the collective memories recorded here of all the participants will give our readers an insight into the 15th FC, ably steered by its formidable chairman.

One last closing thought. I cannot but express my gratitude to my secretariat team members who provided such fantastic support in the writing of our reports. Some of these team members were officers who had served in previous FCs and gave us the benefit of valuable institutional memory. Others were much younger officers—many from the Indian Economic Service, who I recruited as the 'roughs with the potential to sparkle'. My greatest personal satisfaction has been to see many of them turn into diamonds under the high pressures of work and timelines. They are now amongst the best in the world in issues relating to India's fiscal federalism.

A lasting personal satisfaction is that we succeeded in setting up such a strong team of diamonds, who will be available for mining by many future FCs, much beyond India's hundred years of Independence, with the Tricolour fluttering even more majestically outside a future FC Secretary's office!

Jai Hind.

◆

Arvind Mehta was the secretary of the 15th FC.

FALLING IN LOVE WITH AN IDEA

Stories Close to the Heart

Gita Mehta

Where do I begin to tell the story of my journeys with the 15th FC?
To say it was wonderful would be trite and to say that it was a once-in-a-lifetime experience would be stating the obvious. My dear husband, Arvind Mehta, joined the post of secretary to the 15th FC on 12 October 2017. Between April 2018, and January 2020, the FC travelled the length and breadth of India and I (lucky me!) was part of many of those travels.

On 5 April 2018, we took a plane ride to Guwahati and we were on our way to our first port of call, Arunachal Pradesh, India's north-easternmost border state. From Guwahati we flew in a chopper over the vast expanse of the Brahmaputra River, which flowed through the plains and green vales of this beautiful hilly area.

The Arunachalis are a people of several tribes and subtribes, each with a distinctive dress and culture. The museum at Itanagar was fairly illustrative of the same. Primarily nature worshippers, they are fast developing to keep up with the rest of the world. Our stay at the impressive residence of the governor was pleasant. Their greenhouse had a myriad varieties of orchids and other flowers, indeed a sight for sore eyes. It is customary to pray to the gods before embarking on a journey. So we made our way to the Kamakhya Temple in Guwahati on our return from Itanagar. The blessings of Goddess Kamakhya were imperative for the success of the Commission.

As I write, a kaleidoscope of memories fills my mind: the monsoon rain lashing against the coasts of Kerala and Tamil Nadu, the snow-capped mountains of Uttarakhand, the architectural marvels that were the temples. As we were to discover, during our successive visits to each of the states, the gods beckoned and we presented ourselves dutifully to pay obeisance and be blessed. The Padmanabhaswamy Temple, the Guruvayur Temple, the Meenakshi Temple, Lord Jagannath at Puri, Lord Balaji at Tirumala, Maa Kaali at Dakshineshwar, Goddess Ganga at the Gangotri temple, the Parashuram Temple on the banks of the Lohit river in east Arunachal Pradesh, Maa Jawalamukhi Mandir in Himachal, the Siddhivinayak Ganpati Mandir in Mumbai, the Kal Bhairav and Kashi Vishwanathji in Varanasi, the churches, the gurudwaras and a synagogue—the list seems endless. It would not be an exaggeration to say that the journey turned out to be a veritable pilgrimage.

Early morning flights were the norm and sometimes we had to start even earlier, much before sunrise, as in when we were granted the privilege of being present for the Abhishek of Vishwanathji in Varanasi. Late nights too were inevitable when we were being regaled by the chief minister of Nagaland and his Cabinet with popular Hindi numbers and the chairman recounting interesting anecdotes. The performance by the Shillong Choir left us spellbound; we wished the evening wouldn't end. The percussionists at the Jodhpur cultural evening enthralled us with their exquisite beats and sounds.

Naya Raipur would have done Le Corbusier proud with its well-laid-out township and surprise of surprises, a man-made sanctuary in the very midst of the city, wherein the big cats took one disdainful look at us and got on with their business of lunch. What can we say of the renowned Sabarmati Ashram, where even a full day would not have been enough to soak in the Gandhian vibe.

While in Kerala, Smt. Prem Kumari Ma'am and I decided to pay a visit to the Vivekananda Memorial at Kanyakumari. The travel through narrow meandering roads, lined with thatched huts and the verdant green countryside truly made us believe we were in God's Own Country. Our reward was the majestic rock in the Indian Ocean atop which is built the shrine of India's great Swami Vivekananda. There, I found an utter sense of calm in the meditation chamber. On our way back, we chanced upon a museum housing Raja Ravi Varma's paintings. My cup runneth over, dear reader.

Rajasthan was as delightful as I had imagined it to be: the Mehrangarh Fort's grandeur, the Bandhinis, block printing at Sanganer, the vivid colours in dress, the lac bangles and kadhas, the bustling Jaipur market, all call out for another visit!

We grew up studying about the famed Nalanda University and how it attracted scholars from all over the world. The ruins of that era were a throwback. Rajgir was equally fascinating, it conjured in my mind visions of Lord Buddha teaching his disciples and meditating in the forests. The Buddha Smriti Park (also known as Buddha Memorial Park) in Patna was amazing as was the Ganga river next to the Sri Patna Sahib Gurudwara.

Gangotri, where the young Ganga starts its long and tortuous journey, was resplendent with the surrounding sky-hugging mountaintops. As we paid obeisance to Maa Ganga, the icy winds reddened our faces and our bare feet froze. The ride downhill had us in quiet contemplation of nature in its extreme, inspiring awe.

Mawsynram in Meghalaya has the distinction of being the wettest place in India. The drive up to see the famous seven waterfalls proved to be disappointing, since the mist was too thick to catch even a glimpse of it. But a subsequent trip to a village site fulfilled that promise for us. The flowers at this altitude are a sight to behold.

I had often seen the Vidhana Soudha, in Bengaluru, on TV, so when a tour of the same was arranged for us, I was hugely excited. It would suffice to say that I did not come away disappointed.

Lord Jagannath beckoned and then we found ourselves in Odisha. The Sun Temple at Konark is a testimony to the skills

Falling in Love with an Idea

of Indian architects of the thirteenth century. The sound and light show (which we had the distinction of seeing twice in the same evening, thanks to our diligent officers and members who had not been able to get away earlier from their meetings and had missed the regular show!) only reinforced the feeling of marvel at the craftsmanship of artisans of yore.

Every state we visited acquainted us with young officers who had been tasked with the responsibility of escorting us around. Without exception, these young minds impressed me greatly and I came away feeling that our country was in safe hands. But if I had to choose one state among so many for its precision planning, it would have to be Nagaland. Impeccable timing, smart officers (especially the lady officers) and not a glitch. The chief minister and his wife hosted us warmly at their native village called Touphema Tourist Village. Their tribal dances and colourful attires were a treat to watch. My account would not be complete were I not to mention the 'Made in Nagaland' store, where I bought plenty of contemporary jewellery, which I treasure.

After our first visit to Andhra Pradesh in October 2018, there was a change in government and chief minister at the end of May 2019. Lord Balaji called and we were in Tirumala. Everything and I mean everything about the temple tour made my heart sing: from the kitchens that fed the entire township, to the gigantic pressure cookers and kadhais, to the delicious prasad.

Sikkim, like the rest of the Northeast, is breathtaking in its greenery and beauty. The Rumtek Monastery gives a panoramic view of the entire town. The orchids and adeniums in the orchidarium were a sight to behold.

Those Were the Days

Ladakh was my first experience of travelling to a cold desert: sand, rocks and water bodies, all at high altitudes. We had been warned and advised about the inadequacy of oxygen. Fortunately, most of us did well enough. The monasteries were fabulous as always but what stole my heart was the Pangong Lake, which we reached after traversing roads that go up to altitudes of 17,000 feet. The serene waters of the lake and the breathtaking backdrop of brown mountains are etched in my memory.

How can I not mention the Kochi Metro tour, where we discovered a much-welcome gender parity, i.e., there are several ladies running the show or, the GIFT City in Ahmedabad, where even garbage disposal was monitored through their centralized IT hub?

Speaking of water bodies, Lake Chilika comes to mind. It is a vast expanse of water, which is frequented by migratory birds during the winter months. The cleaned-up Naini Lake in Nainital was a pleasant surprise. Boating in the lake as well as a walk along its periphery took me back to my childhood days. The Loktak Lake in Manipur is one of its kind, with innumerable *phumdis* (masses of vegetation and soil) dotting it. People have actually set up small settlements on the larger phumdis.

Our aerial tour of the Gulf of Mannar and the drive to Dhanuskodi on the Tamil Nadu leg of our travel gave us the opportunity to see breathtaking sunsets. We have a precious picture of some of us trying to 'catch' the big ball of flame in our hands. The memorial set up for President Abdul Kalam in his birthplace, Rameshwaram, was as awe-inspiring as the 'Missile Man of India' himself.

Falling in Love with an Idea

And then it was time for Goa, which is all about beaches, churches (especially the Basilica of Bom Jesus) and actually much more. This time I got acquainted with the Portugese quarters and can now accurately identify a house of Portugese architecture by the rooster and/or soldiers on its roof. Nonetheless, there was a bit of sadness amidst all the cheerful bonhomie. This was our last state visit. The FC would soon get busy with its report writing. As the adage goes, all good things must come to an end and so it was with this chapter of our lives.

We had been one big family, and so having to say goodbye wasn't easy. Before I conclude this chapter, it would only be apt to say a word or two about those whom I have come to cherish especially during our trips.

Our chairman, the charismatic, magnanimous and sagacious N.K. Singh and his wife, Prem Kumari Singh, who is sprightly, gracious and generous to a fault. My frequent companion on these travels, Rita Lahiri, who looks alluring in her tasteful sarees; someone who is wise and discerning. Her husband, Ashok K. Lahiri, my guru from our schooldays, is an erudite and knowledgeable man, who often had us doubling up with his wit. FC Member Anoop Singh is learned and suave; someone who always has a kind word for all. Anita Bajar is high on enthusiasm, vivacious and very kind. Her husband, FC Member Ramesh Chand, is a scholar with special focus on rural India. He is congenial and easy to be with. Ranjana Jha, with a great flair for clothes, is smart and compassionate. Her husband, Ajay Narayan Jha, is a quiet person but with a vast trove of gyaan.

Then there was Chetna Bhatia, who looks elegant in her

great collection of silver jewellery. She is affectionate and good-natured. Her husband, Mukhmeet Bhatia, additional secretary, is always ready for a laugh and forever on the lookout for an early morning game of golf. Smt. Nirmala Kota is confident and a beacon of expertise to technologically challenged people like me. If I had to find the cheapest airfare, Nirmala would be the go-to person. Her husband, Shri Ravi Kota, joint secretary, has a great sense of humour, an impish glint in his eyes and an irrepressible laughter. He is also a troubleshooter par excellence.

I have to mention Smt. Maushumi Chakravarty—someone who is fashionable with an ethnic touch and entertaining. She also has an in-depth knowledge of cuisines from different parts of India. I have to mention a few more people here: Shri Antony Cyriac and his lovely wife Lisha, Shri Bharat Garg and his charming wife Deepika. Then there was Sweta, Shikha and Aditi. My list would not be complete without a special mention of Shri P. Venkat Swamy, who provided invaluable support during my husband's tenure. I am truly grateful to him. My gratitude to Shri Jagdish Wadhwa, for being extremely helpful.

I have indeed been blessed to be a part of this warm and loving family.

◆

Gita Mehta accompanied her husband, Arvind Mehta, on some of the visits.

WALKING DOWN MEMORY LANE

A Mesmerizing Tapestry

Chetna Bhatia and
Mukhmeet Singh Bhatia

The past three years weaved themselves into a beautiful tapestry as the 15th FC moved towards submitting its report and completing its term. It gives us an overwhelming sense of pride and gratitude to have been part of an incredible journey.

One of our most memorable experiences was the spiritual visit to the Venkateswara Temple, also known as Tirupati Balaji Temple, in the hill town of Tirumala in Andhra Pradesh. We were fortunate to be a part of the Sri Venkateswara Suprabhatam, the first and pre-dawn seva performed in the sanctum sanctorum. It unfolded a spiritually moving and visually mesmeric experience. Those early hours of dawn found us in captivity. At that magical hour, when the morning breeze gently rustled through the dew-laden flowering trees, we treaded the silent recesses of our minds in supreme solitude.

Similarly, bowing in reverence, we felt blessed to visit Amritsar's Golden Temple, also known as Sri Darbar Sahib, which is spiritually the most significant shrine in Sikhism. Built around a man-made pool, it was rebuilt by the Sikhs several times when it was destroyed by the Mughal and invading Afghan armies. Maharaja Ranjit Singh rebuilt it and overlaid the sanctum with gold foil. The beating retreat ceremony at the Wagah-Attari border was a sight to behold. The heavy downpour that evening did not dampen our enthusiasm in anyway.

The Bhopal visit was equally memorable and the Bhimbetka rock shelters both fascinated and intrigued us. It is an archaeological site that dates back to the prehistoric Palaeolithic and Mesolithic periods and exhibited the earliest of human life in India. The cave paintings were truly spectacular and breathtaking. During the early morning drive to Ujjain, the roads were strangely silent, still devoid of the smoky, fast-paced, man-made machines. Becoming a part of the morning misty glory at the Shri Mahakaleshwar Temple was an hour of soul-searching where the mind pushed aside the earthly pursuits of the incoming day. Observing the richness of His creation, our soul stirred with an overall awakening at the Omkareshwar Temple on the banks of the Narmada River. The serene surroundings had us spending some precious moments in silence and reinstated that the

Walking Down Memory Lane

morning tranquillity is not meant to be disturbed.

The forested regions of Sikkim exhibited a diverse range of flora and fauna. The Rumtek Monastery, surrounded by flowing streams, was enchanting and meditative. The calm and tranquil surroundings added to the beauty. The pièce de résistance was the Ganga Aarti in the holy city of Benaras. The sight of several priests performing the ritual by carrying deepams and moving it up and down in a rhythmic tune of bhajans is firmly entrenched in our minds.

The months gone by have proved to be an extraordinary journey of enriching experience. Writing this, a flood of memories envelops our entire being. This Commission diary cannot be complete without thanking the chairman, N.K. Singh, and Tiny (Prem Kumari), who exemplified the ethos of graciousness and personal touch with the minutest of details. Finally, we would sum up that from Delhi we all went as individuals but came back as one, happy family.

◆

Mukhmeet Singh Bhatia was the additional secretary with the 15th FC. His wife **Chetna Bhatia** accompanied him on some of the official trips.

A STAGE, UNPARALLELED

The Most Rewarding Stint

Ravi Kota

I vividly remember it was 30 March 2018. I was not happy with my posting as joint secretary, 15th FC. Perhaps it was due to my knowledge of central deputation rules as I worked in the Department of Personnel and Training earlier. Postings in the ministries are treated as Central Staffing Scheme (CSS) and in the Commissions as non-CSS. I expected some CSS posting as I was coming from my cadre state, Assam, to the Centre.

However, after serving in the 15th FC for two years and four months, I must admit that, in my 27-year career, it was by far the most rewarding and incredible part of my job as a civil servant.

I worked in the field and at the Secretariat, both at the state and the Centre. I was principal secretary (Finance) in

A Stage, Unparalleled

Assam before joining the FC. Each of these postings gave me good exposure but exposure limited to the domain of that post only. But the work at a FC connects and works through the whole gamut of governance and culminates in a report submitted to the president. It happens every five years as each Commission ceases to exist after its tenure and a new one is appointed. It was the 15th this time, and I am proud to have been a part of such a historical exercise.

The FC is an institution besieged from all sides of the governance spectrum. Some states slam the FC as little more than an extension of the Centre, pressing macroeconomic stability and compliance to the Fiscal Responsibility and Budget Management (FRBM) Act's targets that demand fiscal restraint from states by ignoring pressing local issues. Some others see it as an unfair distributor of resources to poorly performing states.

The beauty of the FC's work is that it is a time-bound exercise. Its recommendations are primal and inescapable to the federal system. It is a platform where the theory and practice of governance meet each other. It throws you into the giant waves of competing viewpoints and interests that force you to the ultimate sharp edges with a vague centre and then quickly into the opposite side of a sharp centre with vague edges on each issue. It is indeed an intellectual roller-coaster ride that takes you through all the vital aspects of governance within its short and fixed tenure.

Simply put, there is a lot that goes on in the Commission within its tenure. It includes a rereading of provisions of the Constitution dealing with the FC and federal-fiscal issues and even digging up the relevant Constitution Assembly deliberations. It also includes going over the FC reports, starting from the first FC in 1951, again and again. It involves cramming through voluminous budget documents, Comptroller and Auditor General's annual reports, memoranda and a myriad of other reports of the Union and 28 states. One has to study reports by expert bodies, theory and practice of macroeconomics, and reports on public finance of the states, which have immense diversity. Crunching numbers and also capturing the nuances of federal issues that the numbers cannot reveal is part of the job. You also have to go through several iterations of horizontal and vertical devolution of central taxes, and interact with the lowest-level functionaries like ward members at the third-tier of governance or Block Development Officer or the public at large. It was intensive. At the same time, it was very enriching and enjoyable: whether attending presentations by the ministries, the states, Accountant Generals and domain experts, or whether crunching numbers or munching at state dinners.

Even I did not realize how much we were traveling till my 'google maps timeline' popped up to picturize our 14-month hectic travel covering almost all states across the country. One needs to experience it to believe it.

At the end of my tenure, I realized how wrong I was to think that I should have been posted in ministries only. I would have missed this lifetime opportunity. I believe that every civil servant should have the experience on this enormous stage, the FC, or some exposure to it to understand how it plays its role as a Constitutional cogwheel to power through the federal fiscal engine in India.

A Stage, Unparalleled

The 15th FC is unique for many reasons. It did some 'firsts' in the FC's history. It was perhaps possible due to the composition of the 15th FC, which had members of great stature, varied experiences and skills with functional complementarity. The chairman, Shri N.K. Singh, being at the ringside of the government for half a century and as an institution himself, had a happy blend of versatile skills of the Members that breathed life into the title of the 15th FC report.

Member Shri Ajay Narayan Jha is the former finance secretary of India. He has also worked as finance secretary of a state. He has a thorough understanding of the working of FCs as he was the secretary of the 14th FC too. I greatly admired his acumen, which was a rare combination of his genius and intense application. He quickly connected countless dots to come up with a very nuanced argument. He had answers for the whys and wherefores about each of the FCs, from the first one.

Member Anoop Singh, professor at George Washington University, with a distinguished career of more than three decades at the International Monetary Fund (IMF) as director of the Asia and Pacific department, and of the Western Hemisphere department, brought to the 15th FC his invaluable international experience in public finance. He made earnest attempts to enable the 15th FC to play a catalytic role in creating the best public finance management systems in India. Having spent a long time abroad, he was, at times, amused at the elaborate protocols that states organized for the 15th FC. During the state visits, escaping from the protocols, he always managed to explore the food or coffee that he liked. In Kohima, he loved the flavour of Nagaland coffee, a new and upcoming Himalayan coffee that the rest of the world is yet to see in a big way.

Further, Member Dr Ashok K. Lahiri is, in my view, a public finance all-rounder. He has immense experience, thanks to his career of about four decades in many roles such as a teacher, head of the National Institute of Public Finance and Policy (NIPFP), senior economist in the IMF, chief economic advisor of India and executive director of the Asian Development Bank (ADB). It was amazing to see his network of students in the civil service of every state that we visited. He was always restless looking at the tardy pace of development and wished for positive change in the system. Deeply devotional and religious at a personal level, Dr Lahiri knows almost everything about ancient Indian temples. So, he was a great company during the state visits to explore temples, and we managed to see many of them: from Gangotri to Rameshwaram and Kamakhya to Siddhi Vinayak. Dr Lahiri ensconced himself in cultural firmament and befriending people. Keeping the 15th FC's mandate in mind, he was unabashed enough to ask pointed questions in any forum, either within the Commission or outside.

Member Prof. Ramesh Chand, also a member of the NITI Aayog, is an agriculture expert. He also has proven abilities to work with both professionals and practitioners, smoothing over a cultural rift that often exists in government. He chose to intervene in the 15th FC's deliberations only when it was necessary. He could quickly study any social setting with the skills of 'reading the room'. He has a solid understanding of

A Stage, Unparalleled

the contemporary connection between rural and agricultural India and its macroeconomics.

A very passionate public finance specialist, Shri Arvind Mehta, a career civil servant, headed the Secretariat that served the 15th FC. He joined the 15th FC at a very senior level when his batchmates joined as secretaries in the central ministries. Most senior civil servants look forward to ending their career as secretaries in central ministries, and Shri Mehta's decision to join the 15th FC showed his commitment to the cause. He professionally built the Secretariat by hand-picking an excellent set of young officers from premier services—Indian Economic Service and Indian Audit and Accounts Service (IAAS)—so that they can become assets to future Commissions. He also got quite a few old hands with previous FC experience. His never-ending hunger for number crunching, iterations of horizontal devolution and passion for public finance were astounding. He focussed single-mindedly on the 15th FC's mandate and its timelines and pushed the Commission, at times, *ad nauseam*.

With the above team, in the actions that will shape his legacy, Chairman N.K. Singh tried to do things unconventionally by opening up the Commission for broad-based consultations. He carried along with him the entire 15th FC team to ensure some of the firsts that the 15th FC could do. They were: (a) constituting advisory body for the FC with the who's who in macroeconomics and public finance in India, (b) consulting with individual ministries, (c) actively being involved with the media—print, electronic and social—with a full-time media advisor, (d) taking both the population of 2011 and total fertility rate for capturing demographics in the formula for horizontal devolution, (e) given the uncertainties associated with introduction of the goods and services tax (GST), preparing two reports: one for 2020–21 and another for five years (from 2021–22), (f) preparing two additional volumes of reports: one on states' finances and the other on the Union's finances, (g) bringing out a coffee-table book on the history of FCs, *Legacy of Trust* and (h) more importantly, while facing the formidable challenges arising out of the COVID-19 pandemic, assessing both the Union's and states' finances and proposing devolution for five years.

Chairman Singh has made it fundamental to his ability to see the complex Indian political economy with clarity and nuance. He has always been focused, deliberate and inclusive in his approach. He knew how to cast his narrative with political veterans, senior Cabinet ministers and experienced chief ministers who were familiar with this 'enormous stage'. His savoir faire allowed him to fit in everywhere he went. He was as comfortable with the prominent figures of the art world as he was with economists, industrialists, politicians and media.

Interestingly, the 15th FC never gave less importance to the states with smaller population and economies. Not only that, Chairman Singh steered the 15th FC to reinforce its integrative role by extolling every state's culture and uniqueness. In packed conference rooms filled with the chief minister and their Cabinet colleagues and senior officers of every state, he would extol the state, and signal how important it was for the country.

It was inspiring to see how energetic and meticulous

A Stage, Unparalleled

Chairman Singh was in attending to the finer details of everything—whether setting up the new office, scheduling meetings/interactions with the states, ministries or expert bodies, swiftly communicating on the phone, texting on WhatsApp and conducting the meetings within the Commission and outside or showing adeptness in moving to virtual meetings during the COVID-19 pandemic.

During the state visits, he has been quite caring towards everyone in the team and family members, if any, accompanying them. So was his wife, Madam Prem Kumari Singh. Both of them were very graceful and always affectionate. Many times, the 15th FC, though a constitutional entity, looked more like a family, with spouses of all members and officers spending eventful and memorable times. It was the trademark of our chairman's leadership!

As I dealt with the divisions of states and administration, besides looking after some of the subjects like local bodies, disaster risk management, grants-in-aid, defence and internal security, I worked closely with some of the youngest and the finest civil servants: Swetha Satya, Shikha Dahiya, Aditi Pathak, Mahesh Kumar and many others indirectly. I cannot forget the warm friendship of Additional Secretary Mukhmeet Singh Bhatia and Economic Advisor Antony Cyriac. We worked as a close-knit group with great teamwork. We also shared several lighter moments and laughed heartily on many occasions. In this journey, Media Advisor Maushumi Chakravarty, and directors Gopal Prasad and Bharat Bhushan Garg were also great partners.

Looking back, I feel that the 15th FC, as an entity, had been at its most profound with such an extraordinary team and its grace always shining. The experience acquired in FC is like gold in the hands of civil servants who can contribute to the cause of sound public finance in the country.

◆

Ravi Kota was the joint secretary of the 15th FC.

A FULFILLING AGENDA

New Kind of Responsibility

Antony Cyriac

As the economic advisor to the FC, I had the onerous task of stepping into the shoes of my illustrious predecessors, who were acclaimed fiscal experts. I had not even partially visualized the depth of the responsibility when I was called for it, thanks to the initiative taken by Arvind Mehta, the secretary to the FC, to rope in officers of the Indian Economic Service, and to the generous recommendation made by the then chief economic advisor, Arvind Subramanian. I was lucky to have joined a team of thorough professionals, including Salam Shyamsunder Singh, Parveen Jain, Kandarp V. Patel and later Bharat Bhushan Garg. We had all handled public finance in some form, but none of us was a fiscal expert. The guidance from the erudite Commission and the deeply academically oriented secretary helped. But my being slow in learning things increased the demands on my time. Slowly, we got into the groove, and started contributing.

There are no boundaries to the quantum of technical work that can be done to fulfil the mandate of an FC. Each Term of Reference of the 15th FC could have been addressed in a number of different ways. Of course, the final judgement and decision on each single aspect of the Terms of Reference was the prerogative of the Commission. However, to present different analytical options to the Commission within the confines of India's emerging administrative and survey database, that too, after balancing the needs of the varied levels of institutional development of the Indian states, was quite a challenge, and at the same time, a thrilling experience. The thought that each option presented to the Commission, if eventually approved, would impact the states' finances significantly, added to the depth of responsibility and to the sense of fulfilment.

The 15th FC believed deeply in consultations. We had the widest imaginable range of consultations, involving all tiers of governments in the country, the whole spectrum of political parties, think tanks and academic experts from different fields and varied geographies, trade bodies and financial institutions, foreign governments and multilateral organizations. The finer points emerged in deliberations may have faded into oblivion, but the distilled wisdom that one gained by sitting through the discussions has been a priceless benefit from the association with the FC.

State visits were thoroughly enjoyable and exciting. Left to myself, I am quite a boring traveller, and would hang around

A Fulfilling Agenda

my hotel or guest house after official engagements. But this time, each state visit, accompanying the FC's members, was a great learning experience. The uniqueness of each state of the Indian Union is not limited to their sociocultural distinctions, ethnicity, historical traditions, religious composition and differences in cuisines and attire, but extends to the unique character of political and bureaucratic class of each state, deeply enmeshed in their traditions. The opportunity to listen to the top rung of provincial leadership in India from close quarters was an unmixed blessing. Each of them perceives development quite differently. In general, I am awestruck by the quality and authority of their developmental perceptions and vision.

One could also witness the paradox of development during state visits. Many of our cities are on a standstill during peak traffic hours. For instance, Sikkim is a relatively developed state in terms of standard indicators. The distance between Sikkim's capital, Gangtok, and New Jalpaiguri is around 120 kilometres, which normally gets covered in three to four hours of drive. But if that lone spinal highway gets somehow interrupted, then people may need to be airlifted in times of emergency!

I would like to conclude by narrating an utterly sad experience that I had, on my way to a state capital. While I set out from Delhi, I met a well-mannered, visibly poor youngster in his early 30s. He had come to Delhi all alone for an urgent surgery, but the hospital he went to, did not give him proper attention. Disillusioned, he was on his way back. My friends and I arranged for a train ticket for his rather short journey and requested him to alight at the place where I was also scheduled to reach. I told him that we would coordinate with the state health authorities and arrange for his treatment in the state capital itself. He agreed, but later changed his mind and headed straight to his village.

He reasoned that he would get support from his relatives in the village and get the surgery done somewhere closer. No amount of persuasion worked; he trusted a 'doctor' in his under-developed village, who would 'save his life'. I had serious doubts. In coordination with the state authorities, I got in touch with the government-run medical college in his district headquarters, not far from his village. The institution is of some repute. The empathetic state health authorities and the hospital authorities promised to take good care of him and treat him free of cost.

He agreed first, but later kept insisting to arrange for treatment with the 'doctor' he trusted. I dissuaded him (and his friend, who had also got in touch with me by then), and strongly pleaded with both of them to go straight to the medical college. Then I got busy with meetings of the FC with the authorities of the state. The man was not reachable over the phone the next afternoon. I then rang his friend, who had just come to know that the patient did not go to the medical college. The reason: he was scared that his 'organs would get damaged'. To my greatest shock, I was also informed that he succumbed to his fate and breathed his last, homebound, that very morning.

Shock and grief—and the dreadful thought of whether we could have managed the whole episode differently—gradually gave way to reason. I could perceive the massive challenges of implementing developmental programmes in

A Fulfilling Agenda

rural India. I learnt that the four non-negotiable components of our rural development agenda should be connectivity, health, education and sensitization. The first three are widely understood and articulated of late, but the last one is of paramount importance to ensure success of public interventions. Programmes should be launched with a mass mobilization tapping all local resources and taking them into confidence. Breaking the tangles of superstitions and ignorance is a humongous task.

◆

Antony Syriac was the economic advisor to the 15th FC.

COMMUNICATING THE ESSENCE

Buzz Around the Work

Maushumi Chakravarty

Out of the blue, towards the end of 2018, I got associated with the 15th FC as its media advisor. What I was told would be an additional charge over and above my existing charge, turned out to be an engrossing and learning experience. The consultations with the ministries and experts, and the state visits taught me aspects of governance which were eye-openers.

I was also told that normally the FC is a low-key beat for finance reporters, and media interest would pick up only nearer the time when the Commission's report would get submitted. Thus, I was told that I would have just 'a bit of extra work' for a few months. The gods must have been

Communicating the Essence

laughing. Things turned out to be dramatically different. First, there was a year's extension of the term for the Commission, and second, the Commission would prepare and submit not one but two reports: one for only a year, namely 2020-21, and the other for the five years from 2021-22 to 2025-26. Everything had to be done twice. But, in retrospect, that only turned out to be a double dose of excitement and fun. What a roller-coaster ride it was! This Commission was never out of the news and the mission always was that we should never move out of sight nor out of mind of people who mattered.

The media coverage of the Commission in the states was always amazing. There was heightened news fall before the state visits, as well as during and after. Even in the smallest of states, there was keen media interest, ably whetted by the chairman strategically giving interviews before the visit to the media houses with maximum reach in the states. Thus, when the Commission reached, the local media would be ready and waiting. Every engagement of the chairman and members were focused upon and widely reported. Anything the Commission did was a media event. Any issue that the Commission looked into was news.

The reportage on the Commission was always keenly followed by the chairman, members and officers. They attached much importance to the reports appearing on all matters under their purview. Opinions by experts were discussed and debated in the Commission's meetings. This mutual respect between the Commission and the media made the former a very nice place to work in.

As activities picked up steam in the Commission, the media discovered that this 15th FC would require sustained interest as the news fall out was huge and continuous, and more new things were being added to the Commission's Terms of Reference. The media reportage picked up pace, especially, as they got easy access to correct and substantive information in the form of media briefings, interviews and press conferences. This, in fact, is how this Commission stood apart from the others till now. The news flow was steady and uninterrupted, and the media sentiments were positive throughout the Commission's tenure. Total transparency ensured that there were no negative comments on the Commission at all. In fact, I would go a step ahead to say that this Commission's media reports explained the policies and agendas positively.

I consider myself privileged to have got a chance to be associated with the 15th FC family.

◆

Maushumi Chakravarty was the media advisor with the 15th FC.

PEOPLE AND ECONOMY POWER

When Work Is Pleasure

Bharat Bhushan Garg

Being from the Indian Revenue Service, I have had the opportunity to work both in the field, i.e., with the Income Tax Department and at the Centre. I was posted as an additional commissioner with the Central Board of Direct Taxes (CBDT) before joining the 15th FC. In fact, the 15th FC is the third Commission that I have had the opportunity to work for after the Forward Markets Commission and the Election Commission of India. Working with this Commission has provided me an insight into the complexities and challenges involved in formulating federal fiscal public policy in India. It has indeed been a privilege to work with this constitutional body.

Those Were the Days

Both my work and personal experience with this Commission are also special for the reasons that, amongst other seasoned members like Shri Ajay Narayan Jha, the former finance secretary of India, Dr Anoop Singh, professor at George Washington University, Dr Ashok K. Lahiri, former CEA and a public finance all-rounder, Prof. Ramesh Chand, also a member of the NITI Aayog and an agriculture expert and Shri Arvind Mehta, secretary and a career civil servant, I had the privilege of working and interacting closely with a stalwart and veteran bureaucrat like Shri N.K. Singh, Chairman 15th FC with a Union Cabinet minister rank. Mr Singh is not only a prominent Indian economist, academician, politician and policymaker, but also a thorough gentleman and a human being par excellence. I must commit that to keep up with the work expectations of the likes of him was no mean feat, as his prowess and leadership in the federal fiscal policy matters and polity is well-documented. And it was indeed a challenge to act as a bridge between his office and the Secretariat. However, having survived the onslaught, when one is to look back, it is extremely satisfying.

One of the strongest positives about the working of the FC is that despite the intensive Terms of Reference, it had a fixed tenure and hence the submission of its report had to be a time-bound exercise. Within the given time frame, the Commission had to hold deliberations with the ministers and senior officials at the Union and state government levels. Beyond the governments, it also had to consult other stakeholders. Such stakeholders included economists, financial sector experts, NGOs and think tanks, international financial bodies like the World Bank, the IMF, the Asian

Development Bank (ADB), the European Commission, the United Nations Development Programme (UNDP) and the Organisation for Economic Co-operation and Development (OECD). The list included experts from the IT sector, agriculture, trade and industry, trade unions, civil society and media. Given the large number of stakeholders involved at the state level and the need for ground-level interaction with representatives from local governments, both panchayats and municipalities, the FC had to also travel to each of the states.

Further, given the backdrop of the nationwide lockdown and pandemic conditions during the year 2020-21 and resultant work from home due to staggered office attendance and timings, the duties with the Commission appeared to be a mammoth task and difficult to accomplish, unless well planned. But under the able guidance of the secretary, additional secretary/joint secretary (Administration) and economic advisor, the task was not only accomplished but done rather well.

A special mention must be made of the backstage officers involved in the planning and execution of the various state and field visits and organizing meeting with the various stakeholders. However, these frequent state visits specially involved enormous amounts of liaising on our part too, given the chairman's rank and profile. Resultantly, the hectic parleys with various central and state government authorities for his travel, security and protocol and media arrangements kept us on tenterhooks. Given the tight agenda and schedule of his visits, each visit had to be timed and flawlessly executed, with zero scope for error. Hence, it kept his office on their toes and, at times, gave us sleepless nights too. But then all is well that ends well. With the successful completion of the tenure of the Commission and its timely submission of the report, I personally feel these interactions have helped me grow more patient and understand matters beyond just public finance.

It has helped me understand the importance of clarity in communication. It has also helped me reconnect with my batchmates from different services posted across India. And yes, last but not least, if one is to look back, as a whole, this experience has been very enriching as well as enjoyable, as it has helped me develop camaraderie with my colleagues and to pick new friends too.

◆

Bharat Bhushan Garg was the director, 15th FC.

AN INTELLECTUAL RIDE

Zoom In and Zoom Out!

Kandarp V. Patel

When I arrived in Delhi to take up my assignment with the 15th FC, I had no idea that it would be the experience of a lifetime. The challenge of the job, intellectual rigour and access to enormous wisdom traversing through time and space is truly unparalleled.

Before joining the Commission, I was working in Hyderabad in the cozy comfort of my own department. As a deputy accountant general, my job was well structured, with a large team and a well-established office. When I arrived in Delhi, I observed a lot of hustle and bustle, and that special air of being the national capital. It was a whole new experience on how the seat of government operates. I was frankly overwhelmed and unsettled, transitioning from a laid-back city to the land of power.

I have vivid memories of my first day of joining the FC. I was given just 24 hours to synthesize about 15 highly technical and seminal papers in public finance. That was baptism by fire. Thus, the journey began.

Practically every day of my last 33 months at the Commission was no different from the joining day. I was given particularly challenging tasks like coming up with alternative horizontal formula for sharing the divisible pool of tax revenues of the Centre, or to find India's tax potential, or to assess debt sustainability of governments. The process triggered my intellect in countless ways as I absorbed the enormous wisdom feeding into the Commission from various public policy experts across the country and as I tried to understand the theoretical constructs behind certain practices. It was a privilege to have the grand view of India's fiscal federalism.

Here, I will just mention some of the bigger takeaways for me from this ride.

COLLECTIVE INTELLIGENCE IN PUBLIC POLICY

The Commission consulted diverse stakeholders with varied backgrounds and across geographies for understanding the complexities and challenges in formulating public policy in India. These consultations provided extremely useful insights into the intricacies of the problems and their possible solutions. We met experts, academic researchers, bureaucrats, politicians, businesspersons and civil society organizations, who provided diverse insights and solutions. In the Secretariat, we brought in necessary skills and

An Intellectual Ride

expertise to filter out the noise and synthesize the insights. Through active and deep listening to diverse stakeholders, I have witnessed pluralism in practice.

DRAGONFLY VIEW

Dragonflies have the biological ability to sense different wavelengths of light. Drawing this analogy to the Commission's work, it was intriguing to see every issue from a 360-degree view.

To the common man, it may seem like the Commission looks only at finance and economic matters related to the country's development. However, in reality, it looks at every public policy problem from the constitutional, social, legal, political, cultural, environmental and economic perspectives. The processes at the back end are intricate and often required us to apply the dragonfly's 360-degree view.

ZOOM IN, ZOOM OUT

While looking at the macro picture, the Commission also dived deeper into very localized and specific issues across the country. Complexities of public policy in practice often come alive at the local level. For instance, even when we recommend grants for more than 2.5 lakh rural local governments as one single block, many a time, we deliberated in detailing the issues that may arise at the Gram Panchayat level. While painting the macro picture, the Commission was continuously zooming in and zooming out, addressing both local sensitivities as well as national requirements.

Those Were the Days

> **FUN FACT**
>
> As one may be aware, each Commission deals with humongous amount of data on a variety of things. From fiscal data and national accounts to census, we have looked at almost all the publicly available data on related subjects. Let me quantify this. When I looked at my computer today, I found 2,078 MS Excel files containing more than 8,000 spreadsheets with more than a million data points. One can imagine how many numbers were crunched to arrive at decisions.

Being at the Mecca of fiscal federalism in India was really an invigorating experience. I will always cherish it in times to come.

◆

Kandarp V. Patel was the director, 15th FC.

LEARNING AND UNLEARNING

Many Wonderful Firsts

Aditi Pathak

Joining the 15th FC after my stint at the Ministry of Commerce involved a drastic change in the nature of work that I had to do: I had to deal with the states in India, after having dealt with different countries at the Ministry of Commerce. I was also a relatively recent recruit in government. After spending one and a half years in Commerce, the FC was only my second posting.

Though I had seen Shri Arvind Mehta before in the corridors of the Ministry of Commerce, I never got a chance to interact with him. It was a sunny afternoon when I, along with two of my batchmates from the Indian Economic Service, met Shri Mehta, secretary, 15th FC, for the first time in North Block. I must admit that I was nervous. I was not at all prepared for the interview. One of my batchmates had suddenly dragged me to meet him.

Shri Mehta had a big room facing those of the chief economic advisor and secretary, Department of Economic Affairs. We entered it and saw the view of the beautiful dome-like structure of North Block from his window. And then started the real interview. A very calm and composed Mehta started the conversation, and after two or three lines of general interaction, uttered the golden words: 'You are hired'. It was a deputation and so we got a level up. It was one of the finest days of our work life. We all came back with happy faces and were eager to join the new assignment.

I formally joined the Commission on 1 February 2020. The office was still under construction, but we managed comfortable set-ups for ourselves. I always had the company and support of my two batchmates Shikha Dahiya and Nitish Saini. It made my tenure at the 15th FC fun.

In the beginning, I was allotted nine states to work with, namely, Bihar, Haryana, Kerala, Maharashtra, Punjab, Rajasthan, Tamil Nadu, Uttar Pradesh and West Bengal. As I said, for me, it was a drastic change from the kind of work that I was handling in the Ministry of Commerce. Straight from international trade and world economy, I started working on the economy of Indian states.

In my tenure at the Commission, particularly during my state visits, I learnt many new things. The specific demands of the states, the meetings with chief ministers, ministers and state's officials, representatives of trade and industry, political parties and local government, agricultural experts

Learning and Unlearning

and economists during these visits significantly widened the horizons of my knowledge. The field visits, which provided an opportunity to see the work at the grassroot level and to interact with the public at large, were also very enlightening. It was dramatically different from theorizing from the ivory tower. I have come to believe that an exposure to the FC can be extremely valuable for every young Indian Economic Service officer in the early stages of their career.

At the 15th FC, I had to deal with various aspects of the nine states, as mentioned above. This work included gathering insights and preparing documents, briefs and presentations for the state meetings.

However, there was always a fun element involved in the state visits, especially to those that I visited for the first time after joining the 15th FC.

One such state that I visited for the first time after joining the Commission was beautiful Kerala. We visited the two main cites of Thiruvananthapuram and Kochi. On the Arabian Sea coast, Kerala, with its greenery and backwaters, is a beauty that cannot be expressed in words. It has some of the world's most famous temples. We visited the famous Padmanabhaswamy and Guruvayur temples. This was also the first time that I got a chance to informally interact with the entire FC team. The chairman, members and secretary always had a pleasant disposition and a smile on their faces. It was always fun learning from them during field visits.

Ashok K. Lahiri in particular was sometimes better than the guides, explaining the facts himself.

Next on my list was Tamil Nadu. Thanks to the FC, that trip was one of the best experiences of my life. Tamil Nadu is much more than Chennai alone. Madurai and Rameshwaram are beautiful sights. One of my best experiences was a visit to the town of Dhanushkodi, only 24 kilometres away from Sri Lanka.

The highway to this town, flanked by the Bay of Bengal on one side and the Indian Ocean on the other, is an experience in itself. When you reach the southern tip and experience the waves, it is a heavenly feeling.

In Bihar, after the regular meetings with the state government and other stakeholders, the Commission got a chance to visit the oldest school of knowledge, Nalanda, which showcases the ancient Indian tradition in education. The recently rebuilt Nalanda University is a modern centre of Buddhism, and today imparts education related to ancient Pali script and the Buddhist religion.

Though relatively small, Punjab is a state truly rich in its tradition and heritage. It offers a mix of everything: from pilgrimage in the Golden Temple to the heightened sense of patriotism at the Attari-Wagah Border, Jallianwala Bagh and Partition Museum. The BSF personnel marching at the Attari-Wagah border during the lowering of the flag ceremony left me spellbound with their sheer brilliance. The ceremony lasted for almost an hour. It left me with a strong feeling of national pride. I loved my visit to Punjab, so much so that I am eager to visit it again.

On our visit to Rajasthan, the state offered one of the grandest welcomes. The cultural heritage of Rajasthan is rich and carefully nurtured and has been sustained over centuries by waves of settlers, ranging from the Harappan civilization to the Aryans, Bhils, Jains, Jats, Gujjars, Muslims and Rajput aristocracy. Rajasthani arts and crafts have emerged as an essential part of the people's lives. Unique in concept, colour and workmanship, the art and handicrafts of the state are beyond comparison. The folk music and dances of Rajasthan are exciting and compelling, the latter is a spectacle of life and colour. Authentic Rajasthani jewellery have caught the fantasy of people everywhere.

The Commission visited the pink city of Jaipur and Jodhpur. It was my great privilege to meet the Maharaja of Jodhpur.

My entire stint at the Commission was a great learning experience; I learnt much from my seniors. This posting moulded me in several ways. I now personally feel more mature and confident while dealing with official matters.

This Commission has been my second home and, in fact, sometimes more than a home. It has provided me memories for a lifetime. Apart from the learning acquired during the state visits, I distinctly remember the series of memorable lunches, birthdays and other get-togethers.

The Commission, in a nutshell, is an amalgamation of people from varied streams and hence a melting pot of different ideas, temperament and diverse knowledge. It gave me an opportunity to broaden and enhance my knowledge on several topics. The presentations made by academicians and practitioners on a variety of issues and themes were thought-provoking and enriching.

I cherish the wisdom shared by Hon. Chairman, Hon. Members, Secretary, other senior officers and colleagues during our state visits and other interactions. It was a memorable association, and it was really difficult to bid goodbye to the Commission. I consider myself privileged to have had a chance to be associated with the 15th FC family.

India is a truly diverse country, not just geographically, but also in terms of religion, culture, language and cuisine. However, there is a strong thread of unity binding this diversity that has to be experienced to be understood. It is definitely a country worth exploring. Though these difficult COVID times have restricted movement and travels for now, I sincerely hope times will change for the good and we all will start exploring our beautiful country soon.

◆

Aditi Pathak was the joint director (States and Administration) with the 15th FC.

A LARGER SENSE OF PURPOSE

Grappling with Intricacies

Shikha Dahiya

I joined the 15th FC after two months of its constitution. This was merely 19 months after my first posting. Little did I know that these three years were going to give me learnings and memories of a lifetime. Besides public finance, this new office gave me the opportunity to learn about almost every sector that requires policy intervention. The best part was that the learning came from first-hand interactions with political parties, local government representatives, state governments, trade bodies and with the leading economists and pioneers working in the field.

I was initially asked to coordinate with the 11 Northeastern and Himalayan states (including the erstwhile state of Jammu and Kashmir till it was made a Union Territory). I was really happy and excited to hear this news as I had never visited most of these states and knew very little of them.

My interactions in these states helped me understand them beyond their public finances. I got a chance to know about their economy, people, culture and day-to-day problems that come with a mountainous terrain. In terms of public finances, most of these states have inadequate revenues and high committed expenditure and debt to gross state domestic product (GSDP) ratio. They also struggle with cost disability factors, dispersed population and natural disasters. However, most of them have good socio-economic indicators that are better than the national average. People of these states are vibrant, and full of life and colour. Here, I provide a brief account of the eight Northeastern sisters that gave me a thrilling experience over the last three years.

The first state visited by the Commission was Arunachal Pradesh, also known as the 'Land of the Dawn-lit Mountains' because of its position as the easternmost Indian state. It is the largest among the eight Northeastern states. Its economy is largely agrarian (in terms of employment), and based on the terraced farming of rice and cultivation of crops such as maize, millet, wheat, pulses, sugarcane, ginger, oilseeds, cereals, potato and pineapple. The state has considerable mineral reserves that hold much potential. There is also an enormous possibility for hydropower generation, but the installed hydropower generation capacity of the state is miniscule. The state's location provides opportunities for trade with countries such as Myanmar, Bhutan and China. In spite of being rich in natural resources, the state receives

A Larger Sense of Purpose

negligible private investment. Connectivity remains a major issue. Improved connectivity will also lead to enhanced tourism in the state.

Arunachal Pradesh is the state with the least population density in the country. According to the 2011 Census, it had only 17 people per sq. kilometre compared with 382 for the country. This low population density increases the unit cost of providing basic socio-economic and administrative services in the state. With a small population of 13.84 lakh (according to the Census 2011), Arunachal is in itself very diverse. There are 26 major tribes in the state along with more than 100 minor tribes and each one is different. We were also informed that the state is fast promoting its festivals to showcase its culture and further boost tourism. Some of these are the Tawang Festival, the Orange Festival, the Ziro Musical Festival, the Bascon Organic Festival that celebrates tribal arts and the Mechuka Adventure Festival.

After the main meetings in the state, a brilliant show was put up by the state government showcasing its art forms including the music and dance of various tribes. For field visit, we went to Namsai district, where we got a chance to visit the Golden Pagoda, which is an excellent specimen of Buddhist architecture. The temple is located on a scenic and serene plateau, cut away from the blaring noises of the city.

The second state visited by the Commission was Assam. It borders Arunachal Pradesh, Manipur, Meghalaya, Mizoram, Nagaland and Tripura, and shares international boundaries of 533 kilometres with Bangladesh and Bhutan. It has one of the richest biodiversity zones in the world which consist of tropical rainforests, deciduous forests, riverine grasslands, bamboo orchards and numerous wetland ecosystems. It has abundant mineral resources such as coal, petroleum, limestone and natural gas as well as other minor minerals such as magnetic quartzite, kaolin, sillimanite, iron ore, clay and feldspar. In spite of being rich in natural resources, the state has low per capita income. It also faces the problem of frequent flooding with the mighty Brahmaputra changing its course frequently. This also leads to high maintenance cost of assets in the state.

In Assam, we visited the famous Kamakhya Temple, known to be the oldest of the 51 Shakti Peeths in the country. It is here that Sati's womb fell when Shiva danced with her corpse. We were told that if a person visits the temple once, they need to visit it again at some point of time. And it did happen for us more than twice as most of the flights to the Northeast were connected through Guwahati. There is so much to the Northeast!

We also got a chance to do a short cruise on the Brahmaputra on a rainy day, with good live music playing in the background, which was an experience in itself. We also visited Majuli, the largest floating river island in Asia. We were informed that the island is slowly reducing in size due to erosion. Efforts are being made to save the island by building embankment roads.

The next two Northeastern states we visited were Nagaland and Manipur, which were similar in several ways. In public finance, both face issues such as high debt, committed expenditure and low revenues. Both states have high forest cover, inadequate infrastructure and protracted insurgency, and have performed well in terms of social indicators.

A Larger Sense of Purpose

Nagaland is one of the three states which has a majority of Christian population, the other two being Mizoram and Meghalaya. The state of Nagaland has about 16 major tribes and many more minor ones. We were informed about the traditional headhunting culture of the state as per which the triumph of a tribe was established when it took away the heads of their enemy tribes. Of course, the tradition is no longer relevant.

The state of Nagaland is fast adopting organic practices in agriculture. The state also has some promising agricultural ventures. For example, the quality of coffee it produces is extremely good. The state has a lot to offer in terms of tourism and the agriculture sector as well.

Nagas celebrate various festivals round the year like Suhkruhnye, Yemshe, Sekrenyi, Moatsü, Mong, Bushu and many others. We visited the state just in time for the Hornbill Festival, which is the biggest festival of the state. The festival is a colourful blend of dance, food, games, ceremonies, painting and other forms of artwork of various tribes of the state. The festival has greatly enhanced the brand value of tourism in the state, with people all over the country travelling to the state during 1–10 December every year. The state government was kind enough to give us a glimpse of the famous festival with beautiful dance performances by various tribes, followed by a traditional lunch. Naga food can be really spicy! Naga Chilli, cultivated in this part of the region, is one of the hottest in the world.

In a separate function organized by the state, the chief minister sang a melodious Christmas carol. A lady officer told me that singing comes naturally to every Naga, the only thing that varies is the degree of sweetness in their voices.

After Nagaland, we went straight to its neighbouring state, Manipur. Ninety per cent of Manipur's terrain is hilly, which encircle a small valley at the centre and a tiny valley on its west. About 63 per cent of the state's population lives in the six valley districts which together constitute just one-tenth of the total land area of the state. Manipur is rich in natural resources and has magnificent lakes, beautiful waterfalls and lush green forests.

During the Commission's visit to Manipur, the state government arranged a special show depicting the various art forms representing the unique rituals of the state. We were also lucky to visit the state at the time of the renowned Sangai Festival, which takes place in the month of November and attracts tourists and performers from various parts of the country. Manipur has a very rich culture of fascinating dances, costumes, music and art forms. The most famous dance is perhaps the Raas Leela, a classical Manipuri dance form depicting the eternal love between Radha and Krishna and the gopis' devotion to Krishna. Manipur is also known for its martial arts like Thang-Ta, which makes use of a sword and a spear. It is a beautiful combination of dance and combat forms. Manipuri people are also very fond of music. Some of the famous Manipuri music forms include Khullang Eshei, Pena Eshei and Lai Haraoba Eshei.

Both Sikkim and Meghalaya attract a large number of tourists throughout the year. The state of Sikkim borders Tibet in the north and northeast, Bhutan in the east, Nepal in the west and West Bengal in the south. It is one of the least populous and second-smallest among the Indian

A Larger Sense of Purpose

states in terms of area. However, it is a fast-growing state, with one of the highest per capita incomes and good social indicators. It is known for its biodiversity, including alpine and subtropical climates, as well as being a host to Kangchenjunga, the highest peak in India and the third highest in the world.

The kingdom of Sikkim was founded in the seventeenth century by the Namgyal dynasty and was ruled by a Buddhist priest-king known as Chogyal. It later became a princely state in British India in 1890. In 1973, anti-royalist riots took place, and in 1975, the monarchy was deposed by the people. Sikkim became a part of India with a referendum in 1975.

After the official meetings in the state, the Commission went to see the Rumtek Monastery, while I visited Nathu La with my other colleagues. The soldiers briefed us about the security rounds on the border, harsh climatic conditions and various stories of valour. We were also told about Baba Harbhajan Singh, a patriotic soldier who was martyred in 1965 while carrying essential supplies for the Army. It is believed that he still protects every soldier on that border and warns them about any attack in advance. The soldiers till date carry out various functions such as providing food believing that he is still alive. Coincidentally, we visited the border in 2019, the year of Baba Harbhajan Singh's posthumous superannuation. The soldiers also informed us that in the meetings that take place regularly with the Chinese, a seat is kept vacant for Baba.

I was curious to know what happens to those who do not believe in him. I was told that if you say that loud enough, he might make his presence felt with weird strong energy. I was not bold enough to try that. Later, we visited a shrine built in his memory by the soldiers called Baba Harbhajan Singh's temple, nestled in the midst of beautiful mountains. It was heartening to visit a place that is full of positive vibes created by the faith of the valiant soldiers and their love for a fellow Army man.

Meghalaya (meaning 'the abode of clouds') is one of the most enchanting states in terms of natural beauty. It is blessed with lush greenery, majestic waterfalls and serene lakes. The state has very pleasant weather and is home to the wettest place in the country, Mawsynram. It is blessed with various natural resources. The state with its deposits of coal, limestone, granite, clay and other minerals, has tremendous industrial potential. It is also renowned for its horticultural crops such as orange, lemon, pineapple, guava, litchi, banana and jackfruit and fruits such as plum, pear and peach, which grow in temperate climates. Lakadong turmeric grown in the Lakadong village and its surrounding areas in the Jaintia Hills in Meghalaya has a very high curcumin content and is considered one of the best varieties of turmeric in the world. Meghalaya has started various sectoral missions such as Mission Lakadong, Mission Jackfruit, Mushroom Mission, Muga Mission, etc., to promote these crops. Due to its geoclimatic conditions, the state is well suited for floriculture and cut-flower production.

The capital of the state, Shillong, is known as the city of music. It stood true to its name as we enjoyed an excellent show performed by the famous Shillong Choir. Khasi people love to sing and dance and are known to enjoy life to the fullest.

A Larger Sense of Purpose

Our visit to the state of Mizoram was rather short. I learnt that it has a single city of Aizawl, which is also the capital. It faces problems of congestion and the need to find innovative solutions. The state is hilly and remote but has strategic importance for national security as well as geopolitical and economic influence in South Asia. It shares 722 kilometres of international border with Bangladesh and Myanmar. An improvement in infrastructure will increase the competitiveness of local goods for exports to its neighbouring countries.

As the duration of our visit was short, we did not really get a chance to go around. However, the state put up a superb cultural show with song-and-dance performances. The voices of the people were melodious and touching and the dance performances were truly mesmerizing.

Tripura is the third-smallest state in India and has a long border with Bangladesh. With its good internet connectivity, it has the potential to develop as an IT hub in the Northeast. It has a full-fledged airport and road density of 1,815 kilometre per 1,000 sq. kilometre as against the national average of 952.8 kilometre/sq. kilometre. In addition to air connectivity, if Tripura can establish a sea link through Bangladesh, it can become a trade gateway linking India and the Northeast to the Association of Southeast Asian Nations (ASEAN).

With eight of the 10 historical monuments of the Northeast in Tripura, the state has ample scope for developing tourism. As the state has unique dance forms and music, it is also culturally very rich. Folk culture of the tribal and non-tribal people of the state forms the backbone of Tripura's cultural tradition. This is reflected as much in the delicately rhythmic physical movement of the Hoza Giri dance of the Reang tribesmen as in the collective musical recitation of Manasa Mangal or kirtan (devotional songs in chorus) of the non-indigenous.

The Garia dance of the tribals and Dhamail dance of the non-indigenous are two important components of Tripura's rich folk culture. Garia is organized on the occasion of New Year and to worship Lord Garia, while Dhamail on familial occasions like weddings. There are also musical duels (Kabi Gaan) between two rival rhyme-makers on public platforms.

Having been associated with these beautiful states, understanding the people, their cultures and their unique challenges and opportunities gave me a fresh perspective on unity in diversity that encompasses this country. Given a chance, I would love to work again with the Commission to deeply comprehend the remaining parts of the country.

◆

Shikha Dahiya was the joint director with the 15th FC.

BOTH PROFESSIONAL AND PERSONAL

Best of Both Worlds

Nitish Saini

After serving in the Department of Economic Affairs for close to two years, I always knew that working with the FC is a lifetime opportunity for those eager to excel in the field of public finance. As soon as the 15th FC got established, I, along with two of my batchmates (this batchmate-ship soon transformed into a close friendship during the Commission's journey, with each having the other's back), Ms Aditi Pathak and Ms Shikha Dahiya, applied for the post of deputy director and were soon hired by Secretary Arvind Mehta.

I was assigned the responsibilities of handling one of the three State Pillars in the Commission (covering both land-locked and coastal states: Gujarat, Madhya Pradesh, Jharkhand, Chhattisgarh, Odisha, Karnataka, Andhra Pradesh, Telangana and Goa) and working as an Officer on Special Duty (OSD) to Hon'ble Member, Shaktikanta Das. My learning curve took a great leap forward especially on economic policymaking while working as an OSD to Hon'ble Member, who has a penchant for every minute detail.

The Commission, under the skilful stewardship of Hon'ble Chairman, Shri N.K. Singh, has pushed the traditional frontiers established by previous Commissions and undertaken vast consultations with all three tiers of government: Union government, state government and local bodies as well as international bodies and outside experts before arriving at its recommendations. As part of the consultative exercise of the Commission, I had the privilege of visiting the aforementioned eight Indian states (except Goa).

These eight states can be distributed into three brackets on the scale of development: more developed, developed and developing, enabling easier comprehension of the key factors encouraging or hindering development of a state. Before undertaking visit to a state, lot of data crunching exercise pertaining to fiscal and socio-economic position of the state vis-à-vis other states and the country used to take place in the Secretariat, which used to act as fodder for the visit. Each state I visited is unique in its own way and has had its share of achievements, with practices to be emulated by others, and failures too.

During the visits, almost every state made a case for higher vertical devolution and raising its share in horizontal devolution before the Commission as compared to the previous

Both Professional and Personal

Commission(s). The Commission had a tough act to perform of balancing the requirements of the Union Government vis-à-vis all 28 states, on the one hand and balancing the inter se requirements of 28 states, on the other. Interaction with both political executives and bureaucracy of the state during these visits was a highly enriching experience. After completion of the highly intensive official meetings, the Commission used to undertake some field visits to gain first-hand experience of the unique initiatives undertaken and developmental challenges faced by the state. The Commission also had the opportunity to visit some of the famous tourist and pilgrimage sites during these visits such as Chilika Lake and Shree Jagannath Temple in Odisha, Tirupati Temple in Andhra Pradesh, Nandanvan Jungle Safari in Chhattisgarh and Mahakaleshwar Jyotirlinga and Omkareshwar Temple in Madhya Pradesh, which have left an indelible mark on my memory.

Over a period of time, the Commission had become more like a family particularly due to intensive interaction, both professional and personal, undertaken during these visits. More importantly, the words of wisdom flowed uninhibitedly during these visits and are lifetime treasures. The hospitality offered by the states to the Commission during the visits was par excellence. I was able to forge new friendships and alliances during the short tenure of the Commission, both within the Commission and in the states, which would probably last forever.

◆

Nitish Saini was the deputy director with the 15th FC.

A MEMORABLE TENURE

Face to Face with Vibrant Media

Anshuman Mishra

It was indeed a privilege for me to get an opportunity to work with the 15th FC. The FC is a constitutional body which I had only read about in newspapers and text books. I have vivid memories of my first meeting with the chairman and the secretary. As an officer dedicated to the 15th FC's media and communications requirements, I was a little nervous in the beginning as I was awed by the aura of the Commission.

Working with stalwarts like the chairman and other members of the Commission was always challenging, especially for a media officer. It was especially so in light of its broad Terms of Reference. I always tried to keep the Commission updated about the latest happenings, even though the media is so democratized and decentralized in present times. When I look back at my brief stint with the Commission, I feel satisfied that I could initiate certain processes to streamline media-related activities. In this regard, the establishment of a media wing in the Commission and starting new social media accounts of the Commission were some concrete outcomes which helped in streamlining media engagements of the Commission.

Interacting with Delhi's vibrant media fraternity was a learning experience. The media was ever eager to give due publicity to the Commission's activities. The tone was set right with a briefing to the senior editors of leading media houses. Apart from the Delhi media, which I had to deal with almost daily, I would like to specially mention my visits, as a part of the 15th FC delegation, to Bihar and Andhra Pradesh. Due to specific demands of these states, friends from the media were very enthusiastic about the Commission's visit. The visionary approach of the Commission to interact with agricultural experts and economists during some of its visits was widely appreciated and given huge coverage in the local and national media.

Starting from coordination with the state Department of Information and Public Relations (DIPR) to respective branches of state media and regional Press Information Bureau (PIB) centre ahead of any visit was crucial in managing the media-related affairs smoothly. On top of it, understanding the requirements of the local media and the pertinent issues during a visit in advance, was quite a task which kept the media wing of the Commission continuously busy. The newly created social media accounts were abuzz with activities to keep the engagements high. It is always a

Those Were the Days

challenging task for a media officer who acts in a fiduciary capacity on behalf of the Commission, and especially when matters are politically sensitive.

At the same time, it was a great learning experience for me to understand the nuances of such dynamic situations. There were obviously some trying times but the chairman's wisdom and affable nature helped me sail through. The director general, PIB, Ministry of Finance, also provided great support and guidance throughout to keep the media wing of the Commission well oiled. On top of it, the chairman's personal interest, his nuanced approach and deep understanding of media-related matters were a great support and made my working at the Commission memorable.

The Commission, being the meeting point for officers from different streams, also gave me an opportunity to broaden my horizon and enhance my knowledge and understanding of pertinent issues. The presentations on a variety of issues given by academicians and practitioners were thought-provoking. The ensuing discussions were even more interesting. The presence of a media officer in the delegation was intriguing to many for the initial few months but, considering the importance of managing the media at a time when things are in a flux, it was hailed as a visionary step taken by the Commission.

I cherish the wisdom shared by Hon. chairman, Hon. members, secretary, other senior officers and colleagues during our personal interactions. It would not have been easy for me but for the affectionate guidance and support extended by the officer on special duty and director in the chairman's office. It was a memorable association. I made friends for a lifetime.

◆

Anshuman Mishra was the deputy director (Media and Communication) with the 15th FC.

UNFORGETTABLE THREE YEARS

Techniques and Technicalities

Salam Shyamsunder Singh

On Thursday, 4 February 2021, I received a call from Shikha Dahiya madam, conveying the message from the 15th FC member Ashok K. Lahiri that I should pen down my experience of being with the Commission. I was overwhelmed and immediately started to recollect my memories. I am sharing here my experience of working in the Commission's Secretariat office and about our state visits to Gujarat, Uttarakhand, Nagaland and Manipur.

Before joining the Commission, I worked in the Economic Division of the Department of Economic Affairs, Ministry of Finance. My job was mainly in the nature of preparing economic analysis and a chapter on the services sector for

Unforgettable Three Years

the *Economic Survey*. I was interviewed by a selection board of the 15th FC consisting of M.S. Bhatia, additional secretary, and Gopal Prasad and Jasvinder Singh, both directors, on 9 January 2018. I received a call the next day from Prasad, informing me about my selection. Being a fresher to the Commission, I felt lucky to be selected into the 15th FC as an assistant director on deputation.

For me, January 2018 was perfect for the transition; it was the month that work on the *Economic Survey* had got over. And my long-time boss, H.A.C. Prasad, senior economic advisor in the Ministry of Finance, had also recently retired on superannuation on 31 December 2017. I joined the Commission on 29 January 2018, curious to learn new things on India's fiscal federalism.

In the early days of the Commission, I was briefed by Joint Director Anand S. Parmar and Director Jasvinder Singh about the finance accounts'/Union Budgets' data, the different major head and minor heads of the accounts and also the basic functioning of the Commission.

After a few days, I was posted with my colleague Parveen Jain in the Economic Analysis Unit headed by the economic advisor, Antony Cyriac, IES. We both reported to Kandarp Patel, director, Indian Audit and Accounts Service (IAAS). We were called the Economic Advisor's (EA) Team. In the FC Secretariat, there were eight units, viz. (i) Administration unit, (ii) Union and Coordination unit, (iii) State Unit I, (iv) State Unit II, (v) State Unit III, (vi) EA Unit, (vii) Media and Communication Unit and (viii) Library. All these units were headed by additional secretary/joint secretary-level officers and worked in close coordination with each other. The officers posted in the Union, state units and EA units were considered technical teams.

The nature of the technical teams' job was mainly to prepare reports and make available the required socio-economic and fiscal data/analysis/discussion note as demanded by Commission members on different subjects. The first task assigned to me was to prepare time series data by collating information on various fiscal and socio-economic indicators from sources available in the public domain. While working in the Commission, data comparability across different sources for different states was a big challenge. For the fiscal analysis, finance accounts and budgets were the two sources the Commission relied upon. Sometimes, the Reserve Bank of India (RBI) data were also used to supplement any gaps.

Working in the Commission Secretariat gave me the opportunity to listen to many top domain subject experts, thus enriching my knowledge. Most of the learning we received was from attending the Commission's discussions and debates among its members and domain experts on different themes. The opportunity given to attend such meetings helped in understanding the Commission's functioning and approach. The Commission had also used the WhatsApp group titled 'FFC-Core Group' comprising all the technical teams, including Respected Secretary, to disseminate necessary instructions and share valuable news and information with officials on a real-time basis.

I also shared my knowledge of computer Excel with my senior colleagues, and also learnt many new things from them in the process. I learnt about the underdevelopment index and infrastructure index and how to calculate and update them with the Commission's latest available data. Based on the basic data set of the finance accounts and budgets of states provided by state teams, I learnt how to adjust the data to make them comparable across states. I also learned the normative approach followed to calculate revenue deficit grants by projecting expenditure and revenue for the next five years.

In the process, I also learnt how to forecast macroeconomic variables and calculate house tax potential using National Sample Survey Office (NSSO) unit-level data. My seniors guided me all the time; they were able to identify my strengths and weaknesses in terms of my skills. They motivated me to work on my weak areas. During the tenure of deputation in the Commission, I got the opportunity to attend three training courses in the IMF's South Asia Regional Training and Technical Assistance Centre (SARTTAC), Delhi, on (i) fiscal analysis and forecasting, (ii) managing capital flows and (iii) macroeconomic diagnostics. The knowledge I gained from these courses were useful in discharging my responsibilities in the Commission.

As an interesting exercise, Secretary Arvind Mehta asked all the technical officers in the Secretariat to make a presentation on a model of horizontal devolution, keeping a condition that the inter se share should not deviate more than 15 per cent from the inter se share prescribed by the 14th Commission. Breaking across the line of hierarchy, this exercise gave everyone an equal opportunity and the full freedom to participate in the intellectual discussion. I, along with my colleagues Parveen Jain and Anand Parmar, presented our model on horizontal devolution. Mehta asked us to present what we thought was only for the use of the Secretariat before two Commission members, namely Shaktikanta Das and Ashok K. Lahiri.

Stakeholder consultations and seeking inputs by assigning studies are standard practice followed in every Commission. In this Commission, holding seminars and international conferences with organizations like the IMF, the World Bank, the Organisation for Economic Co-operation and Development (OECD), the UNDP, the ADB, etc., happened for the first time. An advisory council to the Commission for seeking inputs on addressing the Terms of Reference of the Commission, an expert committee on health and a committee to review fiscal consolidation road map were also set up for the first time. The deliberations made in the meetings of such committees were very useful in enriching our knowledge and understanding of fiscal federalism. The Commission had also sanctioned many studies on different themes. For each study, there was a presentation session of their report. Such interactive sessions helped enrich our knowledge. In this Commission, a media and communication unit was also instituted for the first time for better interaction with the media and getting timely feedback on the Commission's works through media report.

Before visiting any state, there was the usual practice of preparing a presentation on state finance by the respective accountant generals of the concerned state. However, in this Commission, the respective state teams' internal presentation was introduced for the first time before making a state visit as a new standard operating procedure (SOP). These two

Unforgettable Three Years

presentations offered a great opportunity to brainstorm on the important issues in the state and identify the state's problems. Any query on issues raised during these presentations was referred to the state for its official clarification and views. The state visit followed this exercise, and during the official meetings with the state government, the details were discussed. Attending such meetings was quite a learning experience.

Let me now share some memories from these state visits. My senior Nitish Saini, deputy director who was handling Gujarat state, briefed me about the state visit protocols. On 22 July 2018, we landed in Ahmedabad (which is UNESCO's World Heritage City). Being my first state visit, I was very excited. In the evening, we visited the important tourist places in the city. The next day, meetings were lined up with state government officials, and representatives of political parties, local governments and trade and industry. There was also a media briefing at Gandhinagar. After listening to the official meeting's deliberations, I came to the logical conclusion that the state has performed well in terms of fiscal indicators and economic growth. Yet, it lacks in performance of human development and other social indicators. Also, the state faces regional inequality. Seeing the industrial development in the state of Gujarat, I wondered whether it could be credited to its coastal advantage. If so, then why can't India's eastern coastal states reap this advantage?

The next day, we went to Lothal, one of the southernmost cities of the ancient Indus–Saraswati Valley Civilization. We could see first-hand the archaeological remains of the Harappa Port-Town. According to the Archaeological Survey of India (ASI), Lothal had the world's earliest known dock, which connected the city to an ancient course of the Sabarmati River on the trade route between Harappan cities in Sindh and the peninsula of Saurashtra. On our way back, we visited the GIFT City, India's first operational smart city and international financial services centre. The government of Gujarat promoted it as a greenfield project. The technology used there is world class. Among the many awe-inspiring features is that of integrated Automated Waste Collection System (AWS). I have seen such an idea on the Internet, but was happy to find it already implemented in the GIFT City. On our return journey, we went to Mahatma Gandhi's Sabarmati Ashram, which was once the home of the Father of the Nation, from 1917 until 1930. It also served as one of the Indian freedom struggle's main centres. Originally, it was called the Satyagraha Ashram, reflecting the movement towards passive resistance launched by the Mahatma.

On 25 July, early in the day, we left for Rajkot by road. On reaching, we visited Aji Dam, which is situated at a distance of about eight kilometres from Rajkot and 450 kilometres from the Narmada River. The dam receives water through the Saurashtra Narmada Avataran Irrigation (SAUNI) Yojana. This Yojana was launched to divert 1 million acre-feet (MAFt) excess flood water of the Narmada allocated to the Saurashtra region by laying a network of pipelines from canals of the Narmada dam project. After this, we also went to the Integrated Command and Control Centre of the Rajkot Smart City project. The way streetlights and traffic signals, to the CCTV cameras were monitored was very impressive. Even the waste-collection vehicles are tracked using the global

Unforgettable Three Years

positioning system (GPS) from the control room. But the user charges collected for the services are very minimal. We also visited the site where the slum rehabilitation project based on public-private partnership (PPP) mode is successfully being implemented in Rajkot—not only without any cost to the exchequer, but in fact generating extra revenue for the exchequer. Such a model for slum rehabilitation can also be implemented in other cities.

Our next visit was to Uttarakhand. We reached Dehradun on 15 October 2018. First, we went to the Forest Research Institute, near the Indian Military Academy, Dehradun. The serene beauty of the place where the institute is located attracts tourists. It is also a common place where movies are shot. We also visited the museum in the institute where we saw different kinds of forest timbers and pests preserved for research and study.

On 16 October, we met with state government officials and various stakeholders. During the meeting, what struck me was the unique problem of outmigration from the villages in the hills.

In the evening, we went to Parmarth Niketan, Swargashram, Rishikesh, which is about 44 kilometres from Dehradun. It is located on the banks of the river Ganga, between Ram Jhula (bridge) and Janki Jhula (bridge). The Ganga Aarti that we attended purified my heart and soul. I felt blessed by Maa Ganga. The ashram, under the aegis of His Holiness Pujya Swami Chidanand Saraswatiji, promotes an initiative to fight climate change.

The next day, we left Dehradun for Nainital by a state aircraft. We landed in Pantnagar, from where we travelled by car to Nainital, which was about 70 kilometres. The travel from Pantnagar to Nainital by road reminded me of the hilly curved roads of Imphal to Kohima. After reaching Nainital, we visited Naini Lake, which is very alluring, clear and well maintained. At noon, the Commission had interactions with the representatives of the tourism industry. There is ample scope for promoting adventure tourism such as paragliding and innovative adventure sports in this part of the country.

Later in the evening, we went to the organic products mela specially organized by the villagers for us. Put up near the banks of Gaula River of the Bhowali Range, the fete showcased the different products planted in the nearby villages. To my surprise, the Manipuri variety of mulberry trees (for nurturing silkworms) grown in Uttarakhand was also showcased in that mela. We also went to the Indo-Dutch Horticulture Technology Centre, where training for different horticulture courses is provided. Next day, we returned to Delhi directly by helicopter.

The visit to Nagaland and Manipur was a combined one. I got the opportunity to visit these two states twice during my tenure in the Commission; first in November 2018 and later in January 2020. On 27 November 2018, we reached Dimapur by an Indigo flight. From Dimapur, we went by a state helicopter and landed in the Assam Rifles Helipad, Kohima. From there, we directly went to the Kohima World War Cemetery, a memorial dedicated to soldiers of the 2nd British Division of the Allied Forces who died in the Second World War at Kohima, in April 1944. The soldiers died on Garrison Hill's battleground in the tennis court of the deputy commissioner's residence.

Unforgettable Three Years

On 28 November, we had a number of official meetings lined up. During the meetings, one point raised by state officials was that of the 16 Point Agreement signed between the Government of India and the Naga People's Convention, under which the state of Nagaland was created. Point 11 of the 16 Point Agreement mentions that 'to supplement the revenues of Nagaland, there will be need for the Government of India to pay out of the Consolidated Fund of Nagaland, and a grant-in-aid towards meeting the cost of administration'*.

On 29 November, before departing for Imphal, we went to Touphema Eco-Tourism Village. It was a wonderful experience. The warm welcome given to us by the villagers touched our hearts, which I cannot express in words. All the villagers, including from the neighbouring villages, had gathered there to welcome our team led by Hon'ble Chairman N.K. Singh. In the open amphitheatre, a cultural programme was organized to showcase the dances of different tribal communities of Nagaland.

We reached Imphal on the afternoon of 29 November. Our Manipur visit was short, with only official meetings being the highlight. However, in the evening, we saw the Sangai International Festival, a cultural festival organized annually by the government of Manipur to showcase the unique dances of the different communities. The next morning, before meeting with state government officials, I with my two

---

*'The 16 Point Agreement between the Government of India and the Naga People's Convention,' 26 July 1960, https://peacemaker.un.org/sites/peacemaker.un.org/files/IN_600726_The%20sixteen%20point%20Agreement_0.pdf. Accessed on 4 October 2021.

colleagues went to Moirang to see the Indian National Army (INA) Memorial, Loktak Lake and the Keibul Lamjao National Park. However, due to fog in the morning and shortage of time, we couldn't enter the park.

I got the opportunity again in January 2020 to visit Manipur and Nagaland accompanying Hon'ble Members Shri A.N. Jha and Dr Ashok K. Lahiri. In the second visit, we landed in Imphal on 3 January. We had a meeting with state officials on the same day. During the meeting, apart from the fiscal and economic issues of the state that were discussed, members of the Commission also suggested the state government to focus on areas like agriculture since the rainfall in the state is above the national average. We visited the remote districts of Senapati, Churachandpur and Ukhrul, spending one day in each of these districts.

Before departing for Senapati on the morning of 4 January, we went to Kangla Fort, which is considered sacred by the Meitei people. After the Anglo-Manipur War of April 1891, the British occupied the fort. It housed the Assam Rifles after the British left India. It was only in 2004 that the Assam Rifles vacated this fort. After this, we went to Senapati for interactions with district officials. On our return, we visited the Orchid Research and Development Centre in Hengbung which conducts genetic research on different varieties of orchids. Next day, in Moirang, we went to Churachandpur, where we visited the India Peace Memorial Museum, Maibam Lokpa Ching, the INA Memorial, Loktak Lake and the Keibul Lamjao National Park.

My parental house is in Moirang, on the national highway passing Churachandpur. We dropped in for a cup of tea.

Unforgettable Three Years

During the Second World War, Moirang was the headquarters of the INA. Colonel Shaukat Malik of the INA hoisted the Tricolour for the first time on liberated Indian soil on 14 April 1944. The INA Museum at Moirang is a replica of the Singapore INA Memorial, which displays wartime relics and photographs mainly of Netaji Subash Chandra Bose and the INA.

We also visited Loktak Lake, the largest freshwater lake in the entire Northeast. The view from the Sendra Hilltop was breathtaking. Then we went to the Keibul Lamjao National Park on the Loktak Lake, the world's only floating national park. It is the last natural habitat of the sangai (cervus eldii), the dancing deer of Manipur. Though I was born in Moirang, I never got the chance to see sangais in their natural habitat. At Churachandpur, we had meetings with district officials where we discussed issues related to the district and the village councils' functioning. We also visited the Khuga Dam and the Geljang Resort, which is a man-made resort created on the Khuga dam water reservoir.

The next day, we visited Ukhrul district, where Member A.N. Jha was once posted as the deputy commissioner. There, we had a discussion with district officials on the problems being faced by them and the areas of potential development in the district. We also went to see the Shirui Hills.

On 7 January, after interactions with the representatives of local bodies in the morning, we went to Shree Govindaji Temple, which is a major attraction for pilgrims and tourists. In the afternoon, the members met the chief minister of Manipur. After that, we went to inspect the Jawaharlal Nehru Institute of Medical Sciences. Later in the evening, we visited a model village named Langei in Imphal east and Mary Kom's boxing academy in Imphal west.

The next day, we left for Kohima by helicopter. We went to see the Kohima War Cemetery first and then visited the Nagaland State Museum which showcased the tradition and culture of the different tribes of the state. We had a meeting with state officials the same day. On 9 January, we went to the Khonoma Eco-tourism Village and Dzuleke village, a heavenly place surrounded by mountains and small streams with breathtaking views. On returning from the village, we also visited the Jakhama Army Camp. On 10 January, we returned from Kohima to Dimapur via road and then from Dimapur to Delhi by an Indigo flight. After visiting these states, I realized that connectivity is a major problem, and the tourism sector can become an engine of growth in the region provided connectivity and logistics are augmented.

The COVID-19 pandemic has resulted in unconventional approaches of working following new norms such as work from home and organizing virtual meetings and conferences. Despite all these challenges, the final report was submitted on 9 November 2020 by Hon'ble Chairman of the Commission to the president of India. Then, Secretary Sir also superannuated on 30 November 2020.

It was a great experience to hear Secretary Sir speak. After his retirement, he visited the Commission office on 4 January 2021, in keeping with his vision of grooming new talent for the future. He shared his experiences at the Commerce Ministry, where he steered several trade negotiations with our neighbouring countries, the World Trade Organization (WTO) and the Regional Comprehensive

Economic Partnership (RCEP). He shared several thought-provoking ideas on how we can utilize India's foreign exchange reserve optimally to promote exports and, given its strategic importance in the region's latest development of geopolitics, enhance project exports.

WINDING UP, FINALLY

From December 2020, I have been posted in winding up the cell, facilitating the winding-up process of the FC. I had never worked in the Administration Section before, so I was reluctant. However, I saw it as an opportunity for learning and so happily took up the responsibilities. The winding up cell was headed by Shri Bharat B. Garg, director, Indian Revenue Service. Under his esteemed leadership and support from senior colleagues, all the tasks related to the winding up cell were accomplished smoothly. The term of the winding up cell was extended for another 15 working days till 19 February 2021. All the files of the Commission, after proper binding, were transferred to the Finance Commission Division (FCD) of the Department of Expenditure. Then the inventory of stocks such as files, books and computers were moved to the Department of Economic Affairs. The issuing of relieving orders to officers and transferring the service books to the respective departments were also completed. In the meantime, I also received an office order for my new posting in the Sustainable Finance & United Nations section within the Bilateral Cooperation and Sustainable Finance division of the Department of Economic Affairs. I left the Winding Up Cell of the Commission on 19 February, with happy memories.

Those Were the Days

Summing up, working in the 15th FC gave me valuable learning experience not only in office work but also in understanding different states, their geographies, cultures, languages and food habits—experiencing unity in diversity.

I am very thankful to all my seniors and colleagues for their love and affection and their help in my delivering the work assigned by the Commission. It was indeed a memorable three years which I will cherish forever.

◆

Salam Shyamsunder Singh was the assistant director with the 15th FC.